BOSS IT FOR ENGLAND

Kane's already proved he's ready to lead The Three Lions' attack, but if he keeps banging in the goals for his country he could be England's number nine for years to come! How's that for motivation?

ROCK AT EURO 2016

What better way to end the season than ripping it up at the Euros in France? It'll be Kane's first major tournament with the senior England team, so he'll be desperate to show everyone how good he is!

DID YOU KNOW?

Kane had loan spells with Leyton Orient, Millwall, Norwich and Leicester before making it as a first-team regular with Tottenham!

BAG THE GOLDEN BOOT

The striker hit 21 Prem goals in 2014-15 and finished as runner-up in the Golden Boot race behind Sergio Aguero! If he can bust a few more nets this season, there could be a new goal king in town!

YOUR SHOUT!

Will 2016 be Kane's year? Tell us what you think right now on MATCH's Facebook page!

THE GREATEST STRIKEFORCE

EVER!

MATCH checks out the stats that prove BARCELONA trio LUIS SUAREZ, NEYMAR and LIONEL MESSI are the most lethal attack of all time!

HAHA! SCORED AGAIN!

122
They scored more combined goals last season than any strikeforce in Spanish history!

81
That's how many La Liga goals the lethal trio scored in total last season!

70%
MSN bagged 122 of Barcelona's 175 goals in 2014-15!

2014-15 ASSISTS
MESSI	26
SUAREZ	20
NEYMAR	8

STARS' CARS!
Check out these flash wheels and the footy heroes who drive them!

SILVA
Bentley Continental
0-60 3.6 seconds   Price £150,000

NEYMAR
Audi R8
0-60 3.2 seconds   Price £137,500

INSIDE!
YOUR AWESOME MATCH ANNUAL 2016!

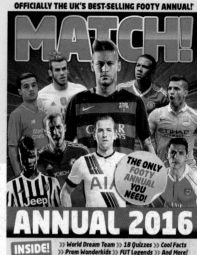

OFFICIALLY THE UK'S BEST-SELLING FOOTY ANNUAL!

MATCH!

THE ONLY FOOTY ANNUAL YOU NEED!

ANNUAL 2016

INSIDE! » World Dream Team » 18 Quizzes » Cool Facts » Prem Wonderkids » FUT Legends » And More!

BIGGEST EVER BUST-UPS 70

FOOTY SUPERHEROES 8

WIN TOP PRIZES 12, 50, 53 & 95

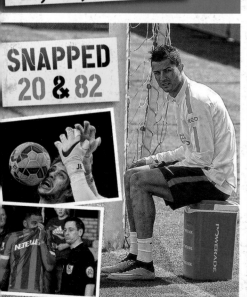

SNAPPED 20 & 82

WORLD DREAM TEAM 38

STARS AS KIDS 64

SUBSCRIBE TO MATCH – TURN TO PAGE 86 FOR MORE INFO!

THE YEAR OF KANE!

MATCH reveals how lethal **TOTTENHAM** goal king **HARRY KANE** can totally own 2016!

FIRE SPURS TO A TROPHY

Tottenham have an awesome squad and, with Kane up front, they've got a striker who can find a way to score against the toughest defences! If Harry can get goals in the biggest games, Spurs could bag their first major trophy since 2008!

KANE'S SKILLS

ENERGY	10
FINISHING	9
PASSION	9
CONTROL	8
HEADING	8
POWER	8

THIS IS TOO EASY!

NO-ONE CAN STOP US, MATCH!

27

Messi, Neymar & Suarez hit 27 of Barça's 31 goals as they stormed to their fifth Champions League title!

54

The red-hot strikeforce made 54 assists last season!

2014-15 GOALS

39 NEYMAR
58 MESSI
25 SUAREZ

3

The trio scored more goals between them than every single team in Europe's top five leagues except Real Madrid, Bayern Munich and PSG!

HOW THEY LINK UP!
Find out how this ace combo works!

Messi floats between positions, before cutting inside to go for goal!

Neymar starts on the wing, but drifts into central areas and swaps with Suarez!

Suarez is the perfect No.9 - he makes tons of clever runs and only needs half a chance to bag!

Messi

Neymar

Suarez

TERRIFYING TRIPLE THREATS!
These trios weren't bad either!

Ronaldo, Rivaldo & Ronaldinho

Brazil ★ 15 goals ★ World Cup 2002

These three fired Brazil to World Cup glory in Japan and South Korea!

Henry, Messi & Eto'o

Barcelona ★ 100 goals ★ 2008-09

MSN broke Barça's season goal record set by Henry, Messi and Eto'o!

Ronaldo, Benzema & Higuain

Real Madrid ★ 118 goals ★ 2011-12

This trio set a new Spanish goals record as Real won the 2011-12 La Liga title!

Ronaldo, Rooney & Tevez

Man. United ★ 79 goals ★ 2007-08

It's no surprise The Red Devils won the Prem and CL with this strikeforce!

Muller, Mandzukic & Robben

Bayern Munich ★ 58 goals ★ 2012-13

This combo helped Bayern become the first German team to win the treble!

BENZEMA

Bugatti Veyron
0-60 2.4 seconds   Price £2 million

MESSI

Maserati GranTurismo MC Stradale
0-60 4.5 seconds   Price £110,000

IBRAHIMOVIC

Porsche 918 Spyder
0-60 2.3 seconds   Price £542,000

IF FOOTY STARS WERE... SUPERHEROES!

MARVEL'S LEGENDARY TOUGH GUYS HAVE GOT NOTHING ON THESE SCARY FOOTY STARS!

I'M GONNA TEAR THE PREM TO SHREDS!

COSTA LOVES SMASHING NETS!

NOTHING GETS PAST ME!

GOOGLE ME ON THE WEB!

DIEGO COSTA WOULD BE... HULK!
The Chelsea striker has superhuman strength, and nobody messes with him when he gets angry!

SERGIO AGUERO WOULD BE... WOLVERINE!
Aguero's reflexes are lightning and his attacks are lethal – just like Wolverine's claws!

PHILIPPE COUTINHO WOULD BE... SPIDER-MAN!
Both are agile and have perfect balance! Coutinho's skills tie opponents in knots like Spider-Man's web!

TIM HOWARD WOULD BE... CAPTAIN AMERICA!
The USA keeper is patriotic and his shot-stopping's as indestructible as Captain America's shield!

DID YOU KNOW?
Bournemouth became the 47th club to play in the Prem when they kicked off their season against Aston Villa back in August!

GET ON WITH THE GAME

R U 2 BROTHERS?

VERNON KAY TV PRESENTER

ROBERT LEWANDOWSKI BAYERN GOAL KING

I'M ALWAYS STRETCHING STOKE'S LEAD!

GUNNERS ASSEMBLE!

PETR CECH WOULD BE... IRON MAN!

Both wear solid armour and Cech defends the goal from danger like Iron Man defends the world!

PETER CROUCH WOULD BE... MR. FANTASTIC!

Crouchy stretches his body into impossible positions to head or volley the ball in from any angle!

ZLAT ALREADY HAS A HAMMER!

ZLATAN IBRAHIMOVIC WOULD BE... THOR!

Zlatan has long hair, is Scandinavian and has a right foot as thunderous as Thor's viking hammer!

CELEBRITY FANS!

MATCH reveals which clubs these famous celebs support!

MISS CHERYL!

Cheryl F.-Versini
X Factor judge
Newcastle

Usain Bolt
Jamaican sprinter
Man. United

Prince William
Duke Of Cambridge
Aston Villa

Jessie J
Pop star
Tottenham

Snoop Dogg
Hip-Hop hero
Norwich

Caroline Wozniacki
Tennis ace
Liverpool

Amanda Holden
BGT judge
Everton

Mo Farah
Athletics legend
Arsenal

HUGO LOL-RIS!

The France keeper loves a joke!

"WHICH MANAGER LOVES CROSSING?"

"ARSENE WINGER. ROFL!"

CR IN/OUT OF THIS WORLD

Astronomers have named a cluster of stars after Cristiano Ronaldo! The CR7 Galaxy was formed 13 billion years ago!

SCARECUTS!

SCARECUTS!

Has Inter Milan's Rodrigo Palacio got a caterpillar living on his head?

MATCH! 9

MEMPHIS
THE NEW RONALDO!

Can MAN. UNITED's new star MEMPHIS DEPAY become a Red Devils legend like Ronaldo?

PACE ✓
We'd love to see Ron and Memphis face-off in a 100m race! They're both so rapid it'd be tough to call, but we'd be tempted to go for the Holland superstar!

DRIBBLING ✓
Both players are masters at running with the ball at their feet, so they're not afraid to take on a whole bunch of defenders!

FREE-KICKS ✓
If you haven't seen Memphis unleash a trademark rocket free-kick yet, head over to YouTube and check them out. He might actually be BETTER at them than Cristiano!

SKILLS ✓
Memphis has the technique and the confidence to bust out tricks even in mega-high pressure games – just like Ron!

GOALS ✗
Depay was the top scorer in the Dutch Eredivisie with 22 goals last season, but that was still nowhere near Ron's crazy total of 48 league strikes!

POSITION ✓
Memphis and Ronaldo are both right-footed players who prefer to start out wide on the left, but love getting into the penalty box and busting nets!

MATCH SAYS
Loads of players get called 'The New Whoever', but we reckon if Memphis can add loads more goals to his game, he could be the real deal!

MATCH!
THE BEST FOOTBALL MAGAZINE!

AGUERO

FACTPACK!

Name: Sergio Aguero
Age: 27
Position: Striker
Club: Man. City
Country: Argentina
Strongest Foot: Right
Top Skill: Lethal finishing!
Value: £80 million
Boots: Puma evoSPEED

WIN!

Put your answers on the entry form in Quiz Answers on page 95 for the chance to win a £50 iTunes voucher!

1 True or False? The deadly finisher used to play for massive Portuguese club Porto before he joined City!

2 Aguero bagged four goals in a single Prem game last season, but which team was it against – Chelsea, Hull or Spurs?

3 How many Champo League goals did the awesome City striker score in 2014-15 – one, four, six, eight or ten?

4 Sergio won a World Cup runners-up medal in 2014 – which team beat Argentina in the final?

5 How many Premier League titles has the Man. City hero won during his career – two, three or four?

WIN!

MATCH!
THE BEST FOOTBALL MAGAZINE!

SUAREZ

1 Which Uruguayan city was the Barça superstar born in – Montevideo, Salto, Rivera, Melo or Minas?

2 The lethal hitman's past teams include Liverpool, Ajax, Nacional and which other Dutch club?

3 He's scored six Prem hat-tricks, but three were against the same team – can you name that club?

4 How many goals did the awesome Uruguay striker score at Brazil 2014 – two, three or four?

5 Which trophy hasn't he won – Eredivisie, Premier League, Copa del Rey, La Liga or Copa America?

Two more for the cabinet!

That's how to pose with a trophy!

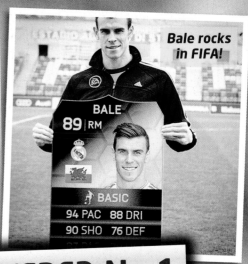

Bale rocks in FIFA!

BALE
89 | RM

BASIC

94 PAC   88 DRI
90 SHO   76 DEF

SUPERSTARS UNCOVERED No.1
BALE

On the Wales team plane!

Catching up with Becks!

This IS Bale, honest!

Nice collection there, Gaz!

We love the Xmas jumper!

Gaz plays a round of golf with his pals!

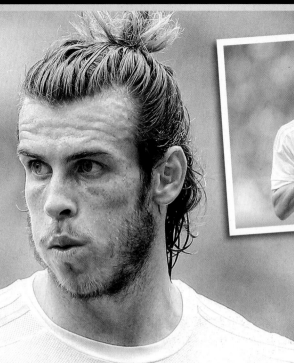

Real Madrid paid £85.3 million to sign Bale in 2013, which is the biggest transfer fee of all time!

85

GOAL-DEN HEART!

He's trademarked his famous 'Eleven of Hearts' celebration to use on his own merchandise!

3

The Wales ace scored in the 2014 Champions League, Copa del Rey and Club World Cup Finals. Wow!

SCHOOL STAR!

His PE teacher gave him rules to make it fair when playing footy - he could only take one touch and his left foot was banned!

SPECIAL MOVE!

THE ROAD RUNNER!

Only the fastest players in the world can do this move, and Bale's one of them! He uses it to burst past defenders and cause chaos!

HOW DOES HE DO IT?

Gaz slowly dribbles and waits for a defender to get really close, then pushes the ball past them and burns away at incredible speed!

BIG MATCH! QUIZ

PREMIER LEAGUE SPECIAL

FLASHBACK!

Which class Chelsea star will want to forget this pic from 2000?

WHO AM I?

Work out the mystery star from these three clues!

↘ I'm a rapid striker who started off in non-league!

↘ I was a non-league transfer record when I signed for my current club!

↘ I made my England debut in 2015!

THE NICKNAME GAME!

Match these Premier League teams with their cool nicknames!

Bournemouth	Sunderland	Man. United	Stoke
1	2	3	4
A	B	C	D
The Red Devils	The Black Cats	The Potters	The Cherries

TRANSFER TRACKER!

Can you fill in the gaps in awesome Arsenal trickster Alexis Sanchez's career?

 2005-06
Cobreloa

 2006-11
?

2011-14
?

2014-
Arsenal

GROUNDED!

Which Prem club plays its home games at this wicked stadium?

Dream Team!

Work out which players are in MATCH's Premier League XI!

Upton Park's Spanish shot stopper!

GK

Liverpool and England right-back!
RB

Swansea legend and Wales captain!
CB

Everton hero and former Blade!
CB

Saints star who made PFA Team of 2014-15!
LB

Norwich's rapid England Under-21 ace!
RW

Man. United and Germany World Cup winner!
CM

Newcastle's Dutch summer signing!
CM

Lightning-fast Watford and Scotland winger!
LW

Lethal Man. City and Argentina hot-shot!
ST

Bournemouth's top scorer in 2014-15!
ST

the PRICE is Right!

Match the stars with the fee their current club paid for them!

1. Schneiderlin — Man. United
2. Clasie — Southampton
3. Amavi — Aston Villa
4. Firmino — Liverpool

A. £25 million
B. £29 million
C. £10 million
D. £8.4 million

Christian Eriksen
Tottenham

Kevin Mirallas
Everton

NAME THE COUNTRY!
What national teams do these awesome stars play for?

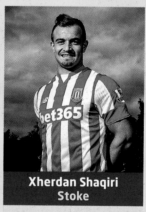
Xherdan Shaqiri
Stoke

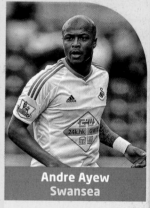
Andre Ayew
Swansea

DERBY RIVALS!

Match up the two teams who call each other 'The Enemy!'

 1. Sunderland
 2. West Brom
 3. Liverpool
 4. Arsenal

A. Tottenham
B. Aston Villa
C. Newcastle
D. Everton

CRAZY KIT!
Which Prem team wore this dodgy away kit in 2010-11?

WICKED WORDFIT!

Fit these 40 Prem superstars into this grid!

Aguero	Defoe	Kane	Rooney
Barkley	Depay	Lukaku	Sanchez
Benteke	Eriksen	Mahrez	Schmeichel
Berahino	Fabregas	Mane	Schweinsteiger
Bojan	Fellaini	Mings	Sigurdsson
Bolasie	Gomis	Mitrovic	Silva
Brady	Grealish	Ozil	Sterling
Cabaye	Hazard	Payet	Stones
Cech	Henderson	Ramsey	Tadic
Costa	Ighalo	Rodriguez	Valencia

Kane

Mes 5

MAHREZ

ANSWERS ON PAGE 95

SNAPPED!
BEST OF 2015! PART ONE

Gomis can't find his ears!

Pull my finger!

It's stink time!

Neymar the ninja!

LVG's got the X Factor!

The Man. United boss is ready to impress Simon Cowell!

High-five, MATCH?

Dawson's stink bomb!

JORDON IBE
Liverpool ★ Winger ★ 19

Reds wonderkid Ibe was playing for Wycombe in League 1 four years ago, but now he's one of the most exciting young stars in the Prem! He's rapid, awesome at dribbling, loves a rocket shot and never stops running - so he's really similar to Man. City star and former Liverpool ace Raheem Sterling!

TOP FIVE SKILLS

SPEED										9
DRIBBLING										8
CROSSING										7
SHOOTING										7
VISION										7

HE'S THE NEXT...
RAHEEM STERLING

NABIL BENTALEB
Tottenham ★ Midfielder ★ 20

Last season, Bentaleb showed why loads of footy experts have tipped him to become a big footy star in the future! His clever, no-nonsense displays in the middle of the park made him a first-team regular for Spurs, and he started every group game for Algeria at the 2014 World Cup. Watch this space!

TOP FIVE SKILLS

SKILL										Rating
PASSING										9
FOOTY BRAIN										8
CONTROL										7
DRIBBLING										7
TACKLING										7

HE'S THE NEXT...
DANI ALVES

HE'S THE NEXT...
MICHAEL CARRICK

ERKIDS!

HECTOR BELLERIN
Arsenal ★ Right-back ★ 20

Ex-Barcelona youth team star Bellerin has the potential to be one of the best right-backs in the world! He broke into Arsenal's first team last season and seriously caught the eye with his expert defending and lightning-fast attacking runs! We can't wait to see a lot more of the awesome full-back in 2016!

TOP FIVE SKILLS

SKILL	RATING
SPEED	9
WORK-RATE	9
TACKLING	8
CROSSING	7
DRIBBLING	7

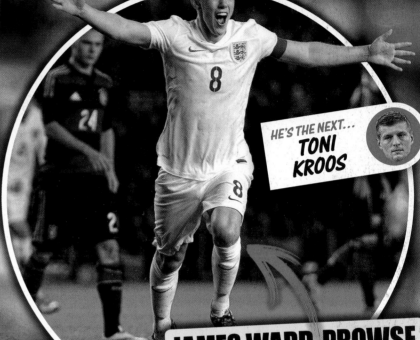

HE'S THE NEXT... TONI KROOS

JAMES WARD-PROWSE
Southampton ★ Midfielder ★ 20

Alex Oxlade-Chamberlain, Gareth Bale and Theo Walcott all came through the Southampton academy, and Ward-Prowse should be the next Saints young gun to hit the big-time! His team-mates love the England Under-21 star for his classy through balls and ace free-kicks – he could be Real Madrid's Toni Kroos in disguise!

TOP FIVE SKILLS

SKILL	RATING
FREE-KICKS	9
PASSING	9
CONTROL	8
VISION	8
LONG SHOTS	7

KURT ZOUMA
Chelsea ★ Centre-back ★ 20

Zouma is the ultimate modern-day centre-back – he's clever, calm, quick and bosses strikers with his monster power! The France star, who can also play as a defensive midfielder, is seen as the obvious replacement for John Terry when he retires – and we reckon he's good enough to fill the captain's boots one day!

TOP FIVE SKILLS

SKILL	RATING
POWER	9
TACKLING	9
HEADING	8
SPEED	8
MARKING	7

HE'S THE NEXT... THIAGO SILVA

TURN OVER TO SEE MORE STARS WHO'LL ROCK 2016!

JACK GREALISH
Aston Villa ★ Midfielder ★ 20

Grealish grabbed the headlines with a Man Of The Match display against Liverpool in last season's FA Cup semi-final – he destroyed The Reds' defence with his epic dribbling and awesome close control! We reckon he plays like a right-footed version of wicked Man. City playmaker David Silva!

TOP FIVE SKILLS

CONFIDENCE	9
CONTROL	8
PASSING	8
DRIBBLING	7
VISION	7

HE'S THE NEXT...
DAVID SILVA

HE'S THE NEXT...
SERGIO BUSQUETS

JOHN STONES
Everton ★ Centre-back ★ 21

Everton ace Stones' tough tackling, calm passing and epic footy brain seriously impressed in the Prem last season! The classy centre-back, who can also play at right-back, has the potential to be an England first-team regular for years! Three Lions boss Roy Hodgson should definitely pick him for Euro 2016!

TOP FIVE SKILLS

FOOTY BRAIN	9
MARKING	9
PASSING	8
TACKLING	8
POWER	7

HE'S THE NEXT...
SERGIO RAMOS

HE'S THE NEXT...
THEO WALCOTT

NATHAN REDMOND
Norwich ★ Winger ★ 21

Redmond burst on to the scene in 2010 for Birmingham, but he's started to make a real name for himself recently for The Canaries! He's always skinned full-backs with his rapid pace and tricky dribbling, but now he's added an end product to his game – like awesome goals! He started the 2015-16 season on fire!

TOP FIVE SKILLS

DRIBBLING	9
SPEED	9
CROSSING	7
FINISHING	7
TRICKS	7

REECE OXFORD
West Ham ★ Midfielder ★ 16

England Under-17 captain Oxford looks like he's been playing in the Premier League for years! His footy brain is massive, his passing totally rocks and he's not afraid of any opponent! The ultra-solid defensive midfielder is comfortable playing at centre-back too, and reminds us of Barcelona legend Sergio Busquets!

TOP FIVE SKILLS

PASSING	8
TACKLING	8
HEADING	7
MARKING	7
STRENGTH	7

BEST OF THE REST...

RUBEN LOFTUS-CHEEK
Chelsea ★ Midfielder ★ 19

Playmaker Loftus-Cheek had a 100% pass completion rate on his Prem debut – his passes are like team-mate seeking football missiles!

BRENDAN GALLOWAY
Everton ★ Left-back ★ 19

Galloway was thrown in at the deep end this season when Leighton Baines got injured, but it didn't faze him. He's got a big future!

JEFF REINE-ADELAIDE
Arsenal ★ Midfielder ★ 17

The France Under-17 hero lit up the Emirates Cup last summer with his silky skills, magical passing and lightning-fast footwork!

JAMES WILSON
Man. United ★ Striker ★ 19

Red Devils gaffer Louis van Gaal picked Wilson ahead of Falcao in some games last season. He's rapid and a good finisher!

DELE ALLI
Tottenham ★ Midfielder ★ 19

Spurs signed the awesome box-to-box midfielder for £5 million in February, and he's got the potential to be a future England star!

PATRICK ROBERTS
Man. City ★ Winger ★ 18

You only need to watch Roberts with the ball at his feet for a few seconds to see he has the potential to go all the way to the top! The England youth star's crossing and dribbling skills are out of this world, plus he's rapid! We can't wait to see how he develops at Man. City if he gets to play lots of first-team footy!

TOP FIVE SKILLS

SPEED	9
DRIBBLING	8
CROSSING	7
FINISHING	7
PASSING	7

HE'S THE NEXT...
ARJEN ROBBEN

With last season's FA Cup trophy!

The Arsenal ace loves dogs!

Chill level maximum!

SUPERSTARS UNCOVERED No.2

SANCHEZ

Hanging out with the world's fastest man!

This must be the coolest bed ever!

Flying with his Arsenal pals!

The Chile star holidays in style!

Give MATCH a lift, mate!

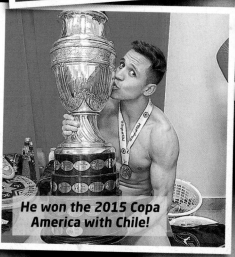

He won the 2015 Copa America with Chile!

CRAZY STATS & FACTS!

35

The rapid goal king, who can play out wide or up front, joined The Gunners from Barcelona for a mega £35 million in 2014!

CUP GLORY!

Sanch is only the second Chilean ever to score in an FA Cup final! He bagged in the 4-0 win over Aston Villa last season!

25

He hit 25 goals in all comps in his debut season - 16 in the Prem, five in the cups and four in the Champo League!

CHILE STAR!

He scored the winning penalty in the 2015 Copa America Final!

SPECIAL MOVE!

THE DIPPING SHOT!

Sanch is a master at unleashing rocket shots that dip at the last minute. They're really tough for even the best keepers to stop!

HOW DOES HE DO IT?

The Arsenal ace uses the top of his foot to strike the ball with serious power, and the spin makes it rise up then dip sharply!

RIO 2 BROTHERS?

Check out these Star Wars footy lookalikes!

CHEWBACCA
HAIRY HERO

THAT'S TOO FAR, MATCH!

ANDY CARROLL
WEST HAM STRIKER

USE THE FORCE, XABI!

OBI-WAN KENOBI
JEDI MASTER

MY BEARD IS WAY BETTER!

XABI ALONSO
BAYERN MIDFIELDER

I WON THE GOAL-DEN BOOT!

C-3PO
HUMANOID ROBOT

ENGAGE ROCKET SHOTS!

NIEN NUNB
MILLENNIUM FALCON PILOT

DO YOU LIKE MY HAT?

JON WALTERS
STOKE STAR

TIME TO BUST OUT THE ROBOT!

JAMES RODRIGUEZ
REAL MADRID ACE

DARTH VADER
SITH LORD

PETR... I AM YOUR FATHER!

PETR CECH
ARSENAL KEEPER

ZLAT NOT LIKE THIS!

WATTO
GREEDY TOYDARIAN

ZLATAN IBRAHIMOVIC
PSG MEGASTAR

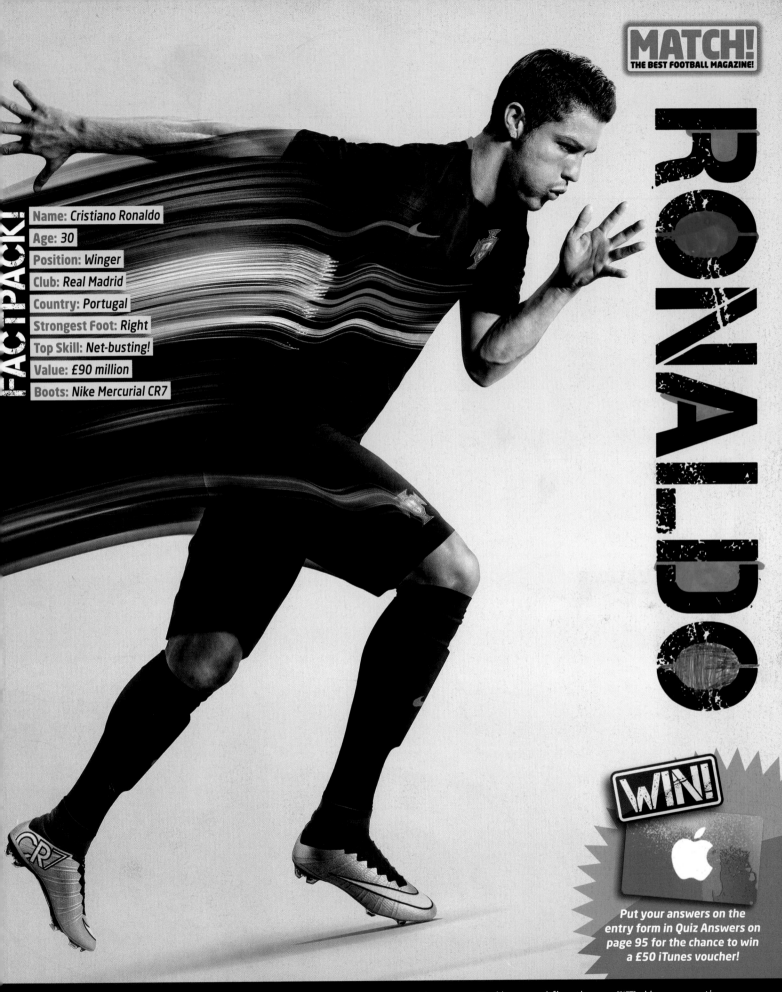

MATCH!
THE BEST FOOTBALL MAGAZINE!

RONALDO

FACTPACK!

Name: Cristiano Ronaldo
Age: 30
Position: Winger
Club: Real Madrid
Country: Portugal
Strongest Foot: Right
Top Skill: Net-busting!
Value: £90 million
Boots: Nike Mercurial CR7

WIN!

Put your answers on the entry form in Quiz Answers on page 95 for the chance to win a £50 iTunes voucher!

1 How many clubs has Ron played for as a full professional uring his career - two, hree, four or five?

2 True or False? CR7 scored more goals with his head than any other player in La Liga last season!

3 How many World Cup goals did the speed demon bag at Brazil 2014 - one, three, five or seven?

4 He scored five times in a single La Liga game last season, but who was it against - Eibar, Getafe or Granada?

5 How many times has the awesome Portugal goal machine won the Champions League?

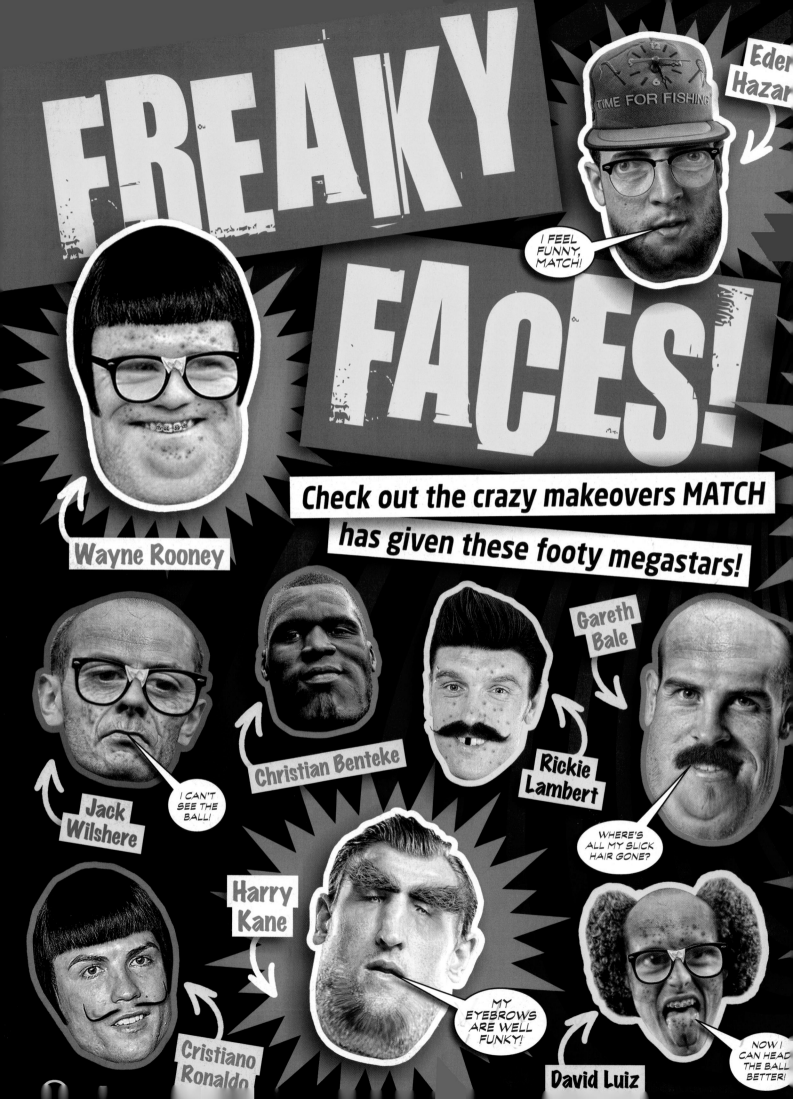

BIG MATCH! QUIZ

FOOTBALL LEAGUE SPECIAL

FOOTY AT THE FILMS!

Name the League 1 star who's hanging out with Paddington Bear in this pic!

5 QUESTIONS ON...

DERBY

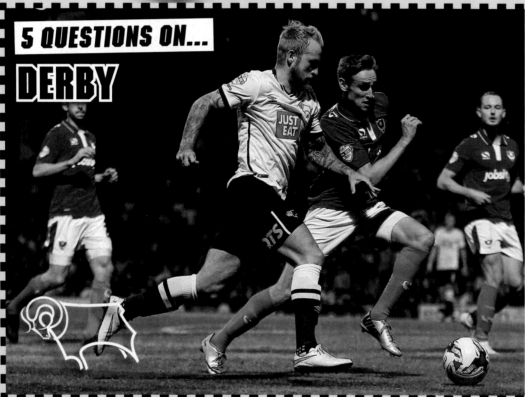

1 How many goals did class striker Chris Martin score in the 2014-15 Championship season - 16, 18 or 20?

2 What's the name of Derby's awesome stadium - Elland Road, Portman Road or the iPro Stadium?

3 What is Derby's nickname - The Rams, The Addicks or The Reds?

4 Which national team does ace forward Johnny Russell play for - England, Wales, Northern Ireland, Scotland or Republic Of Ireland?

5 True or False? Jason Shackell played for Derby in 2011-2012 before re-joining them last summer!

FLIPPED!

Which League 2 beast has had his face messed up in this bonkers pic?

SOCCER SCRABBLE

Rearrange these letters to figure out an awesome Championship team's name!

E D N Y S D L
F N D I
E E A W E
S F H

Football League BRAIN-BUSTER!

How much do you know about the Football League?

1. Man. City and which other current Prem team have won the Championship title the most times?

2. Can you name the oldest club in the Football League?

3. Which Championship goal machine is older – Wolves striker Benik Afobe or Fulham hitman Ross McCormack?

4. True or False? Hull signed midfielder Sam Clucas from League 1 side Chesterfield last summer!

5. Can you name the national team that awesome QPR midfielder Massimo Luongo plays for?

6. Which club plays their home games at the Abbey Stadium?

7. Where did Blackpool finish in the Championship table last season?

8. Which player scored more goals in League 2 in 2014-15 – Matt Tubbs or Reuben Reid?

9. Bristol City, Preston and which other team were promoted to the Championship last season?

10. Which League 2 club is nicknamed The Glovers?

1 ....
2 ....
3 ....
4 ....
5 ....
6 ....
7 ....
8 ....
9 ....
10 ....

ANSWERS ON PAGE 95

CROSSWORD CRUNCH!

Use the clues to fill in MATCH's Football League crossword!

ACROSS

5. Name of Leeds' stadium! (6,4)

8. League 2 champions in the 2014-15 season! (6)

9. First name shared by Rotherham's Buxton and Brighton's Dunk! (5)

14. Republic Of Ireland goalkeeper who plays for Sheffield Wednesday! (6,8)

16. Last season's Championship play-off winners! (7)

19. Wales-based team that plays in the Championship! (7)

20. Derby and Austria goal king, Andreas _ _ _ _ _ _ _! (7)

21. Number of clubs in League 1 that start with the letter 'S'! (4)

22. Derby gaffer Paul Clement was assistant manager at this massive La Liga club! (4,6)

23. Middlesbrough pass master, Grant _ _ _ _ _ _ _ _ _ _! (10)

DOWN

1. Burnley signed Matthew Lowton from this Prem club! (5,5)

2. Preston and Jamaica striker, Jermaine _ _ _ _ _ _ _ _! (8)

3. Shirt number of Dag. & Red. striker Jamie Cureton! (5)

4. Class League 2 team who are known as The Cobblers! (11)

6. The Matchroom Stadium is home to this awesome League 2 team! (6,6)

7. Sports brand who designed Sheffield United's kit this season and make the ACE boot! (6)

9. Bury, Oldham, Port Vale and Shrewsbury play in this epic league! (6,3)

10. Nickname of Ipswich, The _ _ _ _ _ _ _ _ _ _! (7,4)

11. Rapid Birmingham and Wales winger! (5,9)

12. Total number of teams in the Football League! (7,3)

13. Portsmouth signed wicked winger Gary Roberts from this League 1 team! (12)

15. Yorkshire club in League 1, _ _ _ _ _ _ _ _ _ Rovers! (9)

17. Club who lost last season's League 2 play-off final! (7)

18. Championship club who are nicknamed The Royals! (7)

22. Colour of Swindon and Barnsley's home shirts! (3)

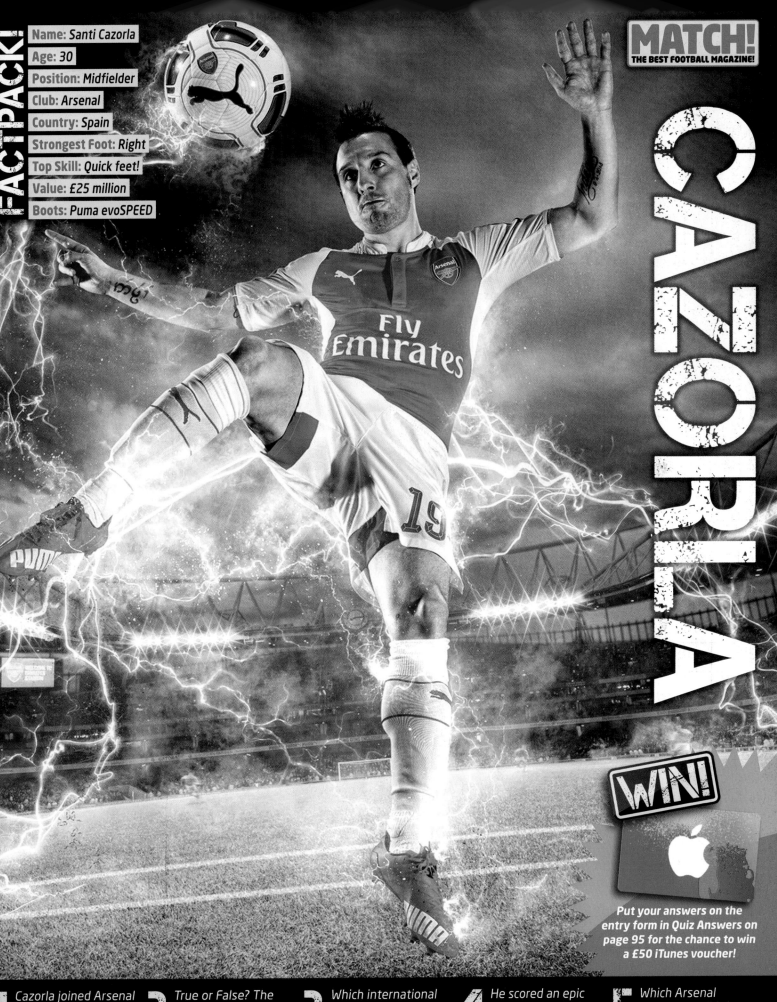

MATCH!
THE BEST FOOTBALL MAGAZINE!

CAZORLA

FACTPACK!

Name: *Santi Cazorla*
Age: *30*
Position: *Midfielder*
Club: *Arsenal*
Country: *Spain*
Strongest Foot: *Right*
Top Skill: *Quick feet!*
Value: *£25 million*
Boots: *Puma evoSPEED*

WIN!

Put your answers on the entry form in Quiz Answers on page 95 for the chance to win a £50 iTunes voucher!

1 Cazorla joined Arsenal for £15 million in 2012 from which massive Spanish team Villarreal or Malaga?

2 True or False? The classy midfielder has played over 70 times in total for his country Spain!

3 Which international tournament hasn't the playmaker won - Euro 2008, World Cup 2010 or Euro 2012?

4 He scored an epic free-kick in which FA Cup final for The Gunners - 2014 v Hull or 2015 v Aston Villa?

5 Which Arsenal team-mate did the Spain megastar play alongside at one of his old La Liga clubs?

Neymar loves a selfie!

He's happy with his new look!

The best attack ever?

SUPERSTARS UNCOVERED No.3

NEYMAR

Check out the VIP tickets!

Cool way to get around, eh?

Who's cooler – Neymar or Becks?

He's starred in Beats ads!

Ronaldo and Neymar – two Brazil legends!

The lethal forward bagged 22 goals in just 29 La Liga starts for Barcelona last season, and made seven assists!

22

WORLD CUP SUPERSTAR!

The trickster was Brazil's best player at World Cup 2014! He was the third top scorer and named in the Team Of The Tournament!

71

Gossips reckon Barcelona signed the 23-year-old for £71.2 million from Brazilian club Santos!

TONS OF TROPHIES!

Since joining Barça he's won La Liga, the Copa del Rey and Champions League. Wicked!

SPECIAL MOVE!

THE FOOT FAKE!

Neymar is one of the best players we've ever seen at faking defenders with fast footwork! He lets them get close, then busts out a move!

HOW DOES HE DO IT?

He slows right down until he stops, then holds his foot over the ball while moving it around – defenders don't know what's coming!

WORLD DREAM TEAM!

Pick your favourite XI from the hottest stars on the planet and, if you match our team, you could win Adidas ACE 15.1 boots and an iPod Nano!

WORLD DREAM TEAM
GOALKEEPERS

THIBAUT COURTOIS
Club: Chelsea ★ **Age:** 23
Country: Belgium ★ **Value:** £50m
Courtois kept 12 clean sheets for Chelsea last season as The Blues won the Prem, and 19 shut-outs the year before as Atletico Madrid bagged La Liga. He pulls off saves some keepers can only dream of!

PETR CECH
Club: Arsenal ★ **Age:** 33
Country: Czech Rep. ★ **Value:** £11m
Cech has kept over 160 clean sheets since moving to the Prem in 2004 – a record only matched by ex-England No.1 David James! The giant keeper joined Arsenal last summer and has already made loads of top saves!

MANUEL NEUER
Club: Bayern Munich ★ **Age:** 29
Country: Germany ★ **Value:** £35m
The Germany No.1 has been the best keeper on the planet for the last few years! His giant frame gives him a big presence in one-on-ones, his decision-making is class and he sweeps up like a defender!

DAVID DE GEA
Club: Man. United ★ **Age:** 24
Country: Spain ★ **Value:** £45m
The unbeatable Spain shot-stopper was United's Player Of The Year in 2013-14 and 2014-15 after making tons of wondersaves! His form last season was mind-blowing, and some of his stops were as good as goals!

MARC-ANDRE TER STEGEN
Club: Barcelona ★ **Age:** 23
Country: Germany ★ **Value:** £22m
Ter Stegen didn't play a single minute in La Liga last season, but he started every Champions League game and starred in the Copa del Rey as Barça won the treble! His agility and reflexes totally rock!

MORE EPIC STARS!
GET A LOAD OF THESE OTHER TOP SHOT-STOPPERS!

HUGO LLORIS
Tottenham
Legendary France captain!

JOE HART
Man. City
Rock-solid England No.1!

GIANLUIGI BUFFON
Juventus
Most expensive keeper ever!

CLAUDIO BRAVO
Barcelona
Barça's reliable La Liga GK!

CHECK OUT YOUR WORLD DREAM TEAM CENTRE-BACKS!
TURN OVER NOW!

WORLD DREAM TEAM
CENTRE-BACKS

SERGIO RAMOS

Club: Real Madrid ★ **Age:** 29

Country: Spain ★ **Value:** £40m

Ramos has bags of pace and awesome technique for a centre-back! He's great in the air too, and often pops up with important goals – like his stoppage-time equaliser in the 2014 Champions League Final!

VINCENT KOMPANY

Club: Man. City ★ **Age:** 29

Country: Belgium ★ **Value:** £32m

Kompany has been one of the best defenders in England since moving to Man. City. His strength, tackling, heading and leadership skills have helped him win two league titles and a Prem Player Of The Season award!

THIAGO SILVA

Club: PSG ★ **Age:** 31

Country: Brazil ★ **Value:** £30m

Silva's right up there as one of the world's best CBs – his power, tackling and heading rock! His £35 million move to PSG from AC Milan back in 2012 made him the most expensive defender ever at the time. Wow!

MATS HUMMELS

Club: B. Dortmund ★ **Age:** 26

Country: Germany ★ **Value:** £35m

Hummels is one of the most complete CBs around, which is why he's always being linked with a move to the Prem! The classy star reads the game so well – you rarely see him having to make sliding tackles!

DIEGO GODIN

Club: Atletico Madrid ★ **Age:** 29

Country: Uruguay ★ **Value:** £24m

The Uruguay captain is a natural leader, and his heading and marking skills mean he's a total nightmare for strikers to play against! He bags the odd goal, too – including the one that sealed the 2013-14 La Liga title!

MORE EPIC STARS!
CHECK OUT THESE OTHER ROCK-SOLID DEFENDERS!

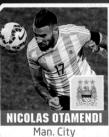

NICOLAS OTAMENDI
Man. City
Ultra-powerful Argentina rock!

RAPHAEL VARANE
Real Madrid
Future world megastar!

GARY CAHILL
Chelsea
No-nonsense England ace!

DAVID LUIZ
PSG
Most expensive defender ever!

JAVIER MASCHERANO
Barcelona
Mr. Reliable at CB or DM!

GERARD PIQUE

Club: Barcelona ★ **Age:** 28

Country: Spain ★ **Value:** £40m

Barça signed Pique from Man. United for just £5 million back in 2008, and that's got to be one of the biggest bargains ever! He's helped them win five La Liga titles, three Copa del Reys and three Champions Leagues!

GIORGIO CHIELLINI

Club: Juventus ★ **Age:** 31

Country: Italy ★ **Value:** £20m

The powerful centre-back is one of the best one-on-one defenders in the world, and proved it last season as Juve made it to the CL final. He's famous for bossing opponents with his strength and aggressive tackles!

JEROME BOATENG

Club: Bayern Munich ★ **Age:** 27

Country: Germany ★ **Value:** £35m

Boateng has come a long way since leaving Man. City in 2011 – he's the first-choice CB for club and country and has won three Bundesligas, the Champo League and World Cup! He's quick, powerful and loves tackling!

JOHN TERRY

Club: Chelsea ★ **Age:** 34

Country: England ★ **Value:** £10m

If the dictionary had the definition of a 'no-nonsense defender', you'd find JT's name next to it! He's one of the best leaders in world footy, and he'll throw his body in the way to stop his opponents from scoring!

LAURENT KOSCIELNY

Club: Arsenal ★ **Age:** 30

Country: France ★ **Value:** £25m

Nobody had heard of Koscielny when Arsenal signed him in 2010, but they know him now because he's one of the Prem's best CBs! His interceptions are class and he pops up with vital goals, too!

MIRANDA
Inter Milan
Powerful and quick Brazil hero!

JAN VERTONGHEN
Tottenham
Mega classy on the ball!

PEPE
Real Madrid
Experienced Portugal CB!

MARQUINHOS
PSG
Rising Samba superstar!

JOSE FONTE
Southampton
Ice-cool Saints skipper!

CHECK OUT YOUR WORLD DREAM TEAM FULL-BACKS!

TURN OVER NOW!

WORLD DREAM TEAM
FULL-BACKS

PABLO ZABALETA

Club: Man. City ★ **Age:** 30

Country: Argentina ★ **Value:** £18m

If you had to describe the perfect full-back, you'd want him to be able to defend and attack, run all day and give 100% in every game – and that perfectly sums up Zabaleta! He's a big Man. City fans' favourite!

MARCELO

Club: Real Madrid ★ **Age:** 27

Country: Brazil ★ **Value:** £25m

Brazil searched for years to find a replacement for the legendary Roberto Carlos after he retired in 2006, but it wasn't until Marcelo became first choice in 2012 that they found him. He's awesome!

DAVID ALABA

Club: Bayern Munich ★ **Age:** 23

Country: Austria ★ **Value:** £40m

Juan Bernat's epic form meant Alaba was mainly used as a midfielder or CB in 2014-15, but that didn't stop him from being awesome! A knee injury ended his season early, but we're sure he'll boss it again in 2015-16!

DANI ALVES

Club: Barcelona ★ **Age:** 32

Country: Brazil ★ **Value:** £15m

Alves is one of the most attacking full-backs ever! He's lightning quick, has top dribbling skills and chips in with ace crosses and rocket shots! He's ripped up La Liga for over 13 years with Barcelona and Sevilla!

BRANISLAV IVANOVIC

Club: Chelsea ★ **Age:** 31

Country: Serbia ★ **Value:** £18m

Ivanovic has got to be up there with ex-Man. United hero Gary Neville as the most consistent right-back in Prem history! He's strong, almost impossible to beat in one-on-ones and loves getting forward to attack!

MORE EPIC STARS!
CHECK OUT THESE OTHER FLYING FULL-BACKS!

LUKASZ PISZCZEK
Borussia Dortmund
Quick, attacking right-back!

RICARDO RODRIGUEZ
Wolfsburg
Seriously speedy Switzerland star!

SEAMUS COLEMAN
Everton
The Toffees' epic attacking machine!

JOSE GAYA
Valencia
La Liga's 2014-15 breakout star!

DANILO
Real Madrid
Real's £23 million new boy!

STEPHAN LICHTSTEINER

Club: Juventus ★ **Age:** 31

Country: Switzerland ★ **Value:** £10m

Seeing Lichtsteiner in our list might surprise you but trust us, he rules! He's won over 70 Swiss caps, has bagged the Serie A title in all four seasons he's been at Juve and is nicknamed 'Forrest Gump' because he never stops running!

NATHANIEL CLYNE

Club: Liverpool ★ **Age:** 24

Country: England ★ **Value:** £15m

Clyne bombs up and down the right wing and has wicked recovery skills, thanks to his blistering pace! After three top seasons with Southampton, he won his first cap for England and sealed a huge move to Liverpool!

JORDI ALBA

Club: Barcelona ★ **Age:** 26

Country: Spain ★ **Value:** £35m

You have to be really good to keep Azpilicueta, Bernat, Gaya and Monreal on the bench, but that's exactly what Alba does for his country! The Barça superstar has pace, energy and loves attacking!

LEIGHTON BAINES

Club: Everton ★ **Age:** 30

Country: England ★ **Value:** £20m

Baines has got more attacking skills than some wingers – he's a lethal crosser, a free-kick expert and packs a thunderous shot! The Three Lions' left-back has got more assists than any other defender in Prem history!

CESAR AZPILICUETA

Club: Chelsea ★ **Age:** 26

Country: Spain ★ **Value:** £22m

Azpilicueta is so good at defending, he switched from right-back to left-back and ended Ashley Cole's Chelsea career in 2013-14. He owns both positions and Mourinho says he's the best left-back in England!

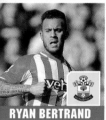

RYAN BERTRAND
Southampton
Prem's best LB in 2014-15!

GREGORY VAN DER WIEL
PSG
First-choice Holland right-back!

LUKE SHAW
Man. United
The Red Devils' £31 million left-back!

JUAN BERNAT
Bayern Munich
Ultra-attacking Spain LB!

DARYL JANMAAT
Newcastle
Magpies assist machine!

CHECK OUT YOUR WORLD DREAM TEAM MIDFIELDERS!

TURN OVER NOW!

WORLD DREAM TEAM
MIDFIELDERS

SANTI CAZORLA

Club: Arsenal ★ **Age:** 30

Country: Spain ★ **Value:** £25m

2014-15 was the season when Cazorla became one of the Prem's best CMs – he totally ran games from a deeper midfield role! He's won two Euros with Spain and is one of the best two-footed players in the world!

ANDRES INIESTA

Club: Barcelona ★ **Age:** 31

Country: Spain ★ **Value:** £40m

Iniesta is one of the greatest midfielders of all time – his footy brain, passing and dribbling are out of this world! He won his fourth Champions League in 2015, and was Man Of The Match in the final!

CESC FABREGAS

Club: Chelsea ★ **Age:** 28

Country: Spain ★ **Value:** £27m

The passing king got 18 assists in 34 Prem games last season, which was seven more than anyone else! Strikers love playing with Fabregas, because they know they'll get bags of chances to score with him around!

PAUL POGBA

Club: Juventus ★ **Age:** 22

Country: France ★ **Value:** £70m

Man. United fans must be gutted they lost Pogba for free in 2012. His power, technique, box-to-box runs and long shots have helped Juve win three Serie A titles and turned him into one of Europe's hottest stars!

JORDAN HENDERSON

Club: Liverpool ★ **Age:** 25

Country: England ★ **Value:** £30m

Three years ago, Liverpool were getting stick for spending £20 million on Hendo and some thought he'd leave Anfield. Now he's The Reds' captain, a first-choice starter for England and a FIFA 16 cover star!

MORE EPIC STARS!
CHECK OUT THESE OTHER MIDFIELD MACHINES!

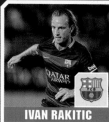

IVAN RAKITIC
Barcelona
Classy CL final goalscorer!

MESUT OZIL
Arsenal
Out-of-this-world vision and passing!

NEMANJA MATIC
Chelsea
Rock-solid man mountain!

XABI ALONSO
Bayern Munich
Legendary passing machine!

TONI KROOS
Real Madrid
Epic Germany pass master!

PHILIPP LAHM

Club: Bayern Munich ★ **Age:** 31

Country: Germany ★ **Value:** £35m

The Bayern legend captained his club to a third Bundesliga title in a row in 2015 and his seventh in total! He used to be one of the planet's best full-backs, but Pep Guardiola has now turned him into a class CM!

KEVIN DE BRUYNE

Club: Man. City ★ **Age:** 24

Country: Belgium ★ **Value:** £55m

Not many players finish seasons with stats like De Bruyne had in 2014-15 – he got 20 league assists! It equalled the all-time Bundesliga record and helped seal a big-money move to the Premier League!

SERGIO BUSQUETS

Club: Barcelona ★ **Age:** 27

Country: Spain ★ **Value:** £35m

If you'd like a solid star to protect the defence in your starting XI, DMs don't come better than Busquets! He's used his positioning, tackling and intelligence to own Barça's holding midfield role for years!

LUKA MODRIC

Club: Real Madrid ★ **Age:** 30

Country: Croatia ★ **Value:** £35m

Real Madrid megastars Bale, Ronaldo and James usually grab the headlines for the Spanish giants, but midfield master Modric is just as important! His defence-splitting passes and class footy brain totally rock!

MARCO VERRATTI

Club: PSG ★ **Age:** 22

Country: Italy ★ **Value:** £40m

We can't believe Verratti's still only 22 years old – he's already a midfield genius! He's been compared to Italy legend Andrea Pirlo because of his jaw-dropping vision, control and passing. He's unbelievable!

YAYA TOURE
Man. City
Ivory Coast's beast CM!

PHILIPPE COUTINHO
Liverpool
Creative Samba playmaker!

B. SCHWEINSTEIGER
Man. United
Red Devils midfield master!

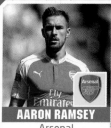

AARON RAMSEY
Arsenal
Box-to-box Gunners goal grabber!

ARTURO VIDAL
Bayern Munich
Chile's midfield powerhouse!

CHECK OUT YOUR WORLD DREAM TEAM WINGERS!

TURN OVER NOW!

WORLD DREAM TEAM
WINGERS

CRISTIANO RONALDO

Club: Real Madrid ★ **Age:** 30

Country: Portugal ★ **Value:** £90m

If you were to design the perfect player, you'd build Ron! He's fast, strong, unstoppable in the air, skilful and a top-class finisher! He's always hungry to rip net, which is why he's scored over 500 career goals so far!

ARJEN ROBBEN

Club: Bayern Munich ★ **Age:** 31

Country: Holland ★ **Value:** £34m

Seeing Robben fly down the wing with his mad pace and crazy dribbling skills is incredible to watch! He hugs the touchline before cutting inside and unleashing rocket shots at goal with his lethal left foot!

DAVID SILVA

Club: Man. City ★ **Age:** 29

Country: Spain ★ **Value:** £45m

There aren't many Prem players MATCH likes watching more than Silva! The classy creative king is nicknamed 'Merlin' because he's a wizard on the ball - his close control, vision and dribbling skills are magic!

ALEXIS SANCHEZ

Club: Arsenal ★ **Age:** 26

Country: Chile ★ **Value:** £45m

Sanchez had a dream 2014-15 - he won Arsenal's Player Of The Year, the FA Cup and Copa America! He's the first Gunners star since Thierry Henry to hit 20 goals in all comps in his debut season!

MEMPHIS DEPAY

Club: Man. United ★ **Age:** 21

Country: Holland ★ **Value:** £35m

Memphis was the Eredivisie top scorer last season with 22 goals, which helped him seal a £31 million move to United! He's called 'The New Ronaldo' because of his sick pace, dribbling and free-kicks!

MORE EPIC STARS!
CHECK OUT THESE OTHER WICKED WIDE MEN!

FRANCK RIBERY
Bayern Munich
The Bundesliga's demon dribbler!

LUCAS
PSG
PSG and Brazil magic man!

JAMES RODRIGUEZ
Real Madrid
World Cup Golden Boot winner!

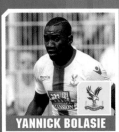

YANNICK BOLASIE
Crystal Palace
Eagles' tricky dribbling machine!

ARDA TURAN
Barcelona
Technical Turkey wing king!

EDEN HAZARD

Club: Chelsea ★ **Age:** 24

Country: Belgium ★ **Value:** £65m

We don't think it'll be long before Hazard's challenging Messi and Ronaldo for the Ballon d'Or! He makes things happen with his epic dribbling skills and acceleration, plus he knows how to bust nets!

MARCO REUS

Club: B. Dortmund ★ **Age:** 26

Country: Germany ★ **Value:** £47m

Reus can play out wide or up front and is one of the Bundesliga's top stars. He's rapid, has great skills and rips nets for fun! He's been linked with a move to the Prem for ages – and we hope it happens in 2016!

GARETH BALE

Club: Real Madrid ★ **Age:** 26

Country: Wales ★ **Value:** £100m

The most expensive footballer ever catches the eye with his explosive style, rapid runs and long shots! He scored in the Champions League, Copa del Rey and Club World Cup Finals in 2014 – he loves big games!

JAVIER PASTORE

Club: PSG ★ **Age:** 26

Country: Argentina ★ **Value:** £37m

Pastore, who joined PSG for a French record fee of £37 million back in 2011, creates tons of chances and scores spectacular goals! Footy legend Eric Cantona reckons he's the best player in the world!

RAHEEM STERLING

Club: Man. City ★ **Age:** 20

Country: England ★ **Value:** £49m

City made Sterling the most expensive English player of all time last summer, and we think he'll be worth every single penny! His electric pace and dribbling skills give defenders nightmares!

THEO WALCOTT
Arsenal
Lightning-quick England ace!

KOKE
Atletico Madrid
Atletico's pin-point pass master!

ANGEL DI MARIA
PSG
Still the Prem's most expensive star ever!

JUAN MATA
Man. United
Silky Spain playmaker!

MARIO GOTZE
Bayern Munich
World Cup final goalscorer!

CHECK OUT YOUR WORLD DREAM TEAM FORWARDS!

TURN OVER NOW!

WORLD DREAM TEAM
FORWARDS

LIONEL MESSI

Club: Barcelona ★ **Age:** 28
Country: Argentina ★ **Value:** £120m

What more can we say about Leo? He's the best finisher and dribbler of all time, plus he's won four Ballon d'Ors, four Champo Leagues and seven La Ligas! He's scored 38 goals or more in all comps for the last seven seasons!

ZLATAN IBRAHIMOVIC

Club: PSG ★ **Age:** 33
Country: Sweden ★ **Value:** £20m

Zlat always wows the crowd with his sick skills, which include no-look passes and crazy wondergoals like backheeled volleys and 40-yard overhead kicks! He's ripped over 160 nets in the last five seasons!

HARRY KANE

Club: Tottenham ★ **Age:** 22
Country: England ★ **Value:** £40m

Goal king Kane had one of the best breakthrough seasons we've ever seen in 2014-15! He ended the campaign with 31 goals in all comps for Spurs and scored on his international debut for England!

ROBERT LEWANDOWSKI

Club: Bayern Munich ★ **Age:** 27
Country: Poland ★ **Value:** £50m

Lewa's a born finisher - if he gets a sniff of goal, the net's gonna rip! The Poland ace was a goal machine in his four-year spell with Dortmund, and he carried that on last season with 17 league strikes for Bayern!

SERGIO AGUERO

Club: Man. City ★ **Age:** 27
Country: Argentina ★ **Value:** £80m

Aguero's an electric striker who comes alive in the penalty box! He's rapid, has defence-destroying skills and loves beating keepers with early shots! He won the Prem Golden Boot last season with 26 goals!

MORE EPIC STARS!
CHECK OUT THESE OTHER RED-HOT HITMEN!

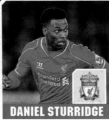

DANIEL STURRIDGE
Liverpool
England's lethal leftie!

ANTOINE GRIEZMANN
Atletico Madrid
France's new goal king!

NEYMAR
Barcelona
Super Samba trickster!

OLIVIER GIROUD
Arsenal
Classy Gunners hitman!

THOMAS MULLER
Bayern Munich
Best footy brain ever?

DIEGO COSTA

Club: Chelsea ★ **Age:** 26

Country: Spain ★ **Value:** £45m

Some people had doubts Costa would be a hit in England after his move from Atletico Madrid in 2014, but he smashed in 20 league goals to fire The Blues to their first Prem title since 2010. Awesome!

WAYNE ROONEY

Club: Man. United ★ **Age:** 29

Country: England ★ **Value:** £30m

Wazza's got passion, a top footy brain and rips nets with all types of strikes – one-on-ones, first-time finishes, headers and free-kicks! He's close to scoring 200 career Premier League goals. Legend!

LUIS SUAREZ

Club: Barcelona ★ **Age:** 28

Country: Uruguay ★ **Value:** £80m

Suarez was on a different planet in his last season for Liverpool, and he was just as good for Barça in 2014-15! He only played 27 league games because of suspension, but grabbed 16 goals and 14 assists!

KARIM BENZEMA

Club: Real Madrid ★ **Age:** 27

Country: France ★ **Value:** £45m

Red-hot finisher Benzema has pace, power, movement and an unbelievable eye for goal! He's one of the best No.9s in Europe and has hit over 130 goals for Real, making him their 11th highest scorer ever!

PIERRE-E. AUBAMEYANG

Club: B. Dortmund ★ **Age:** 26

Country: Gabon ★ **Value:** £28m

Speedster Aubameyang had the best season of his career in 2014-15 after being given the chance to play as Dortmund's main striker. He hit 25 goals in all comps, which included strikes against Bayern and Arsenal!

GONZALO HIGUAIN
Napoli
Argentina net-buster!

JACKSON MARTINEZ
Atletico Madrid
Colombia powerhouse!

EDINSON CAVANI
PSG
Ligue 1's record signing!

CHRISTIAN BENTEKE
Liverpool
Reds' £32.5 million goal machine!

CARLOS TEVEZ
Boca Juniors
Mega passionate goal king!

FILL IN YOUR WORLD DREAM TEAM LINE-UP!

TURN OVER NOW!

WORLD DREAM TEAM
MY FAVE STARTING XI

You've seen MATCH's epic shortlist, now pick your favourite starting XI!

GOALKEEPER

RIGHT-BACK

CENTRE-BACK

CENTRE-BACK

LEFT-BACK

WINGER

MIDFIELDER

MIDFIELDER

WINGER

FORWARD

FORWARD

CLOSING DATE: Jan. 31 2016

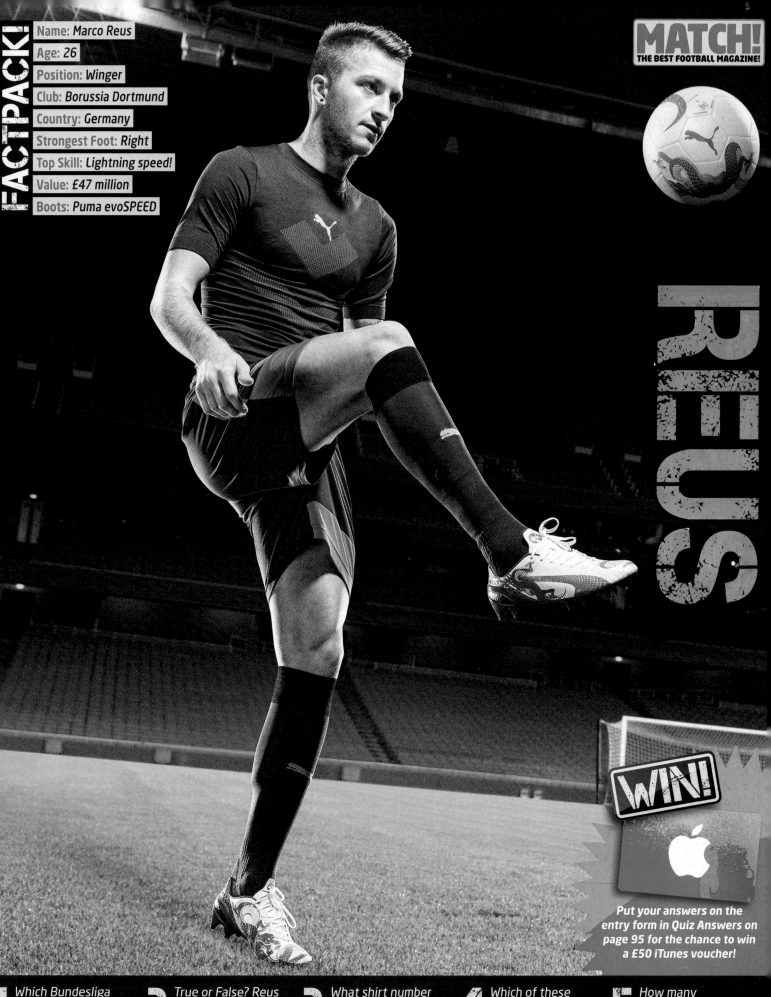

MATCH!
THE BEST FOOTBALL MAGAZINE!

FACTPACK!

Name: *Marco Reus*
Age: *26*
Position: *Winger*
Club: *Borussia Dortmund*
Country: *Germany*
Strongest Foot: *Right*
Top Skill: *Lightning speed!*
Value: *£47 million*
Boots: *Puma evoSPEED*

REUS

WIN!

Put your answers on the entry form in Quiz Answers on page 95 for the chance to win a £50 iTunes voucher!

1 Which Bundesliga team did Dortmund buy Marco from in 2012 - Wolfsburg or Monchengladbach?

2 True or False? Reus scored two goals for Germany on their way to lifting the 2014 World Cup in Brazil!

3 What shirt number does the awesome net-buster wear for Dortmund - No.7 No.11, No.14 or No.16?

4 Which of these countries has Reus scored against for Germany - England, Wales or Republic Of Ireland?

5 How many international caps has Marco won for his country - more than 20 or less than 20?

DESIGN YOUR OWN KIT!

We love doodling new versions of our fave kits, and now we want you to do the same!

Check out some of this season's kits and see how they compare to some of the best and worst ever! Then comes the fun bit! Get your pens out, design some kits on the opposite page (or a piece of paper) and send them to us. The best one wins a Prem shirt!

BEST & WORST NEW KITS?

Barcelona

Man. United

Everton

CD Guijuelo

ALL-TIME BEST KITS?

Holland 1988

England 1990

Barcelona 2011-12

Man. United 1970-71

Lazio 2015

ALL-TIME WORST KITS?

Arsenal 1992-93

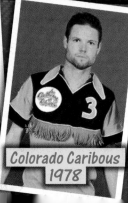
Colorado Caribous 1978

Coventry 1978-79

Hull 1992-93

Athletic Bilbao 2004-05

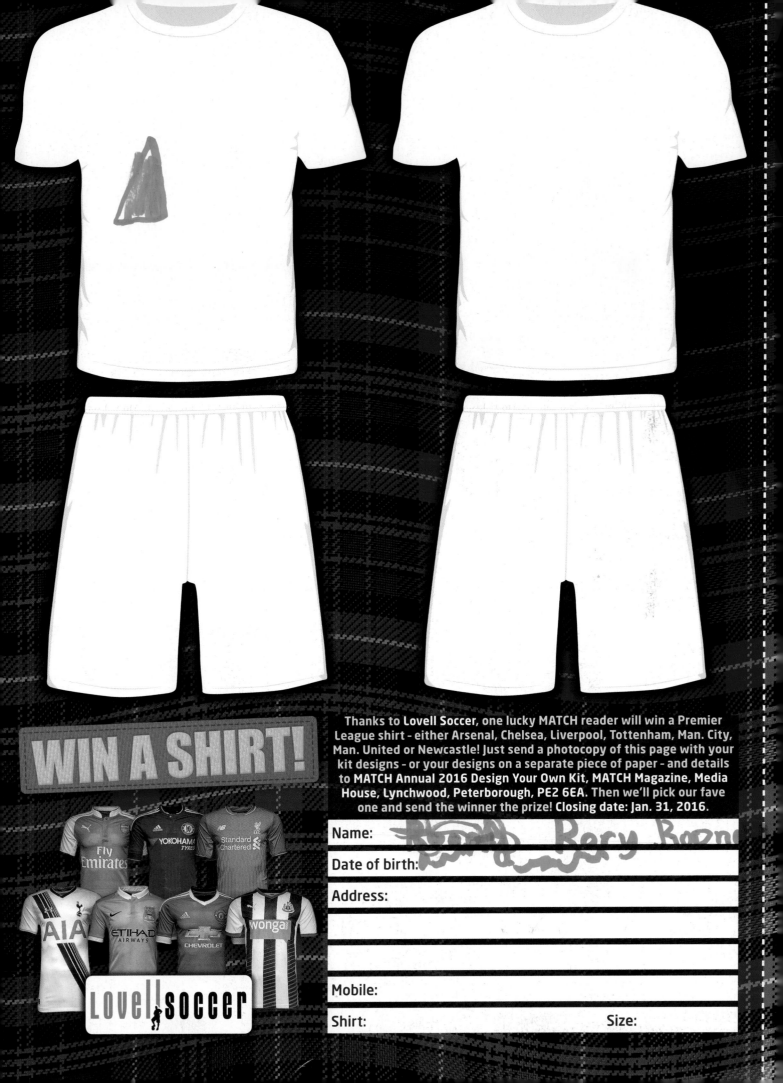

WIN A SHIRT!

Thanks to **Lovell Soccer**, one lucky MATCH reader will win a Premier League shirt - either Arsenal, Chelsea, Liverpool, Tottenham, Man. City, Man. United or Newcastle! Just send a photocopy of this page with your kit designs - or your designs on a separate piece of paper - and details to MATCH Annual 2016 Design Your Own Kit, MATCH Magazine, Media House, Lynchwood, Peterborough, PE2 6EA. Then we'll pick our fave one and send the winner the prize! Closing date: Jan. 31, 2016.

Name:

Date of birth:

Address:

Mobile:

Shirt: **Size:**

Lovell soccer

Eden loves his tunes!

Selfie with Brazil legend Rivaldo!

Is that bag full of old smelly socks?

SUPERSTARS UNCOVERED No.4

HAZARD

Nice hair, Willian!

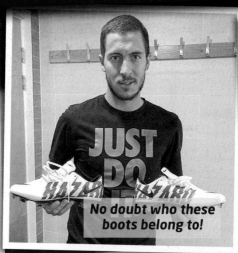

No doubt who these boots belong to!

Hazard makes a new friend!

Has he raided Petr Cech's wardrobe?

Taking on Olly Murs at FIFA!

The Player Of The Year trophy rocks!

CRAZY STATS & FACTS!

Chelsea signed the awesome wing king from Ligue 1 club Lille for £32 million back in 2012!

32

FOOTY FAMILY!

Eden's mum and dad were both footballers, and his bro Thorgan plays for Borussia Monchengladbach in the Bundesliga!

3

Hazard has won three Player Of The Year awards so far in his career – two in Ligue 1 and one in the Prem!

YOUNG STAR!

His local football team in Belgium signed him up when he was just four years old!

SPECIAL MOVE!

THE BODY SWERVE!

Hazard is a master at unbalancing defenders with slick body swerves! They're really hard to read and even tougher for opponents to stop!

HOW DOES HE DO IT?

The Belgium star fakes to go one way with a clever drop of the shoulder, then goes in the opposite direction to totally fool his marker!

10 THINGS YOU NEED TO KNOW ABOUT...
THE ☐🏆☐ EUROS!

EURO 2016 kicks off this summer, so MATCH gives you the ultimate guide to the awesome tournament!

1 MORE TEAMS

Euro 2016 will see 24 nations take part in the finals for the first time in the tournament's history! The first-ever Euros in 1960 was played between four countries, it expanded to eight in 1980 and was doubled again in 1996 to 16 teams!

2 THE HOSTS

France will stage the European Championship for a record third time after they beat bids from Turkey and Italy. The ten host stadiums include Stade de France, Parc des Princes, Stade Velodrome and the brand-new Stade de Lyon!

3 LUCKY STADIUM

Saint-Denis' Stade de France will host the Euro 2016 Final on July 10 – and the hosts will really fancy their chances of victory if they get there. Les Bleus played the 1998 World Cup and 2003 Confederations Cup Finals there – and won both!

4 FAMOUS TROPHY

The European Championship trophy is named after Henri Delaunay, who was the first general secretary of UEFA and came up with the idea of the tournament in the 1950s. The famous cup was redesigned for Euro 2008 to make it even bigger!

6 QUALIFYING RECORD

A massive 53 teams took part in qualifying for Euro 2016 - the largest number ever - with new boys Gibraltar playing in their first official UEFA competition. Qualifying began way back in September 2014 and lasted 15 months!

7 GERMAN GREATS

Germany have made it to the finals of the Euros 11 times, which is an all-time record! They didn't play in any of the first three tournaments, but have appeared in every single one since 1972 and have got to the semi-finals eight times in total!

8 TOP SCORER

UEFA president Michel Platini is the European Championship's all-time top goalscorer! He's bagged nine goals in total - two more than legendary England striker Alan Shearer - and he netted all of them for France at Euro 1984!

9 BONKERS STATS

There will be 51 games at Euro 2016 - 20 more than Euro 2012! It will be shown live in more than 230 countries, and 150 million fans are expected to watch every game with 2.5 million supporters predicted to fill stadiums!

10 MEGA MASCOT

The official mascot for Euro 2016 is called Super Victor, and his name was voted for by fans ahead of Driblou and Goalix. He's a boy with cool super powers and epic footy skills, and he even has his own Facebook and Twitter accounts!

5 SUPER SPAIN

Spain are the defending champions after winning Euro 2012, and are the only country ever to win back-to-back European titles. They'll be aiming to win a record fourth Euros in France, which will see them go one clear of Germany!

NOW TURN OVER FOR OLIVIER GIROUD'S GUIDE TO FRANCE 2016!

OLIVIER GIROUD'S...
GUIDE TO FRANCE 2016!

UEFA EURO 2016 FRANCE

Awesome **ARSENAL** goal machine **OLIVIER GIROUD** gives **MATCH** all the big info on the Euros and host nation **FRANCE!**

HOSTING EURO 2016

GIROUD SAYS: "Playing in an international competition like the Euros in my own country is like a dream come true! France is definitely ready for this, and we're all looking forward to welcoming our international football friends into our country."

PASSIONATE FANS

GIROUD SAYS: "French people are really passionate about football, and obviously we feel their support even more when we play at home. When you're a player in the national team, you really feel the fans behind you and it makes us stronger!"

GREAT SIGHTS

GIROUD SAYS: "Each of the host cities have a lot to offer for tourists. The weather is different from region to region, but in the south the summer is always great. Every city has a different atmosphere and vibe, so it's worth visiting them all!"

FRENCH CUISINE

GIROUD SAYS: "International fans should definitely try the traditional French breakfast - the world famous pain au chocolat! Braver diners should also try escargots, but I wouldn't recommend them to people who aren't experimental!"

Escargots are cooked snails

MEMORIES OF FRANCE 98

GIROUD SAYS: "I still remember watching all the matches with my family, and running through the house celebrating when we won the trophy! I hope that we can bring as much joy and pride to the nation as the team did back then."

FRANCE'S MAIN RIVALS

GIROUD SAYS: "All the teams are strong. Germany have a great team with a lot of confidence, so we need to watch out for them. Spain and Italy probably want to make up for their early exits at Brazil 2014, so they'll also be hard to beat!"

BLEUS STARS TO WATCH

GIROUD SAYS: "We have a strong squad with a good mix of younger and older players. Young players like Griezmann and Pogba are already established at top European clubs, so they'll be two very strong individuals in our team!"

RACE FOR THE GOLDEN BOOT

GIROUD SAYS: "Ronaldo is obviously always a candidate for top goalscorer, or maybe Muller of Germany. Hopefully it'll be a French player, and we can stay in the tournament right until the very end!"

BENZEMA, GRIEZMANN & LACAZETTE

GIROUD SAYS: "Competition can only be positive, especially in a tournament like the Euros where everyone needs to be ready to play at any time. I hope to have a successful season with Arsenal and go into the competition ready to play a big role for the team!"

TEAM-MATES REVEALED!

Giroud gives MATCH the lowdown on his France mates!

THE JOKER
GIROUD SAYS: "Antoine Griezmann."

BEST FRIEND
GIROUD SAYS: "Mathieu Debuchy."

MOST FASHIONABLE
GIROUD SAYS: "Besides me, ha ha! Yohan Cabaye."

WORST DRESSER
GIROUD SAYS: "Stephane Ruffier."

THE STRONGEST
GIROUD SAYS: "Eliaquim Mangala."

DRESSING ROOM DJ
GIROUD SAYS: "Patrice Evra."

BIG MATCH! QUIZ

EURO CHAMPIONSHIP SPECIAL

Belgium	Croatia	Czech Republic	Denmark

ODD ONE OUT!
Which of these countries have never played in a Euro final?

Holland

Portugal

FLIPPED!
Which Wales superstar has had his face messed up in this weird pic?

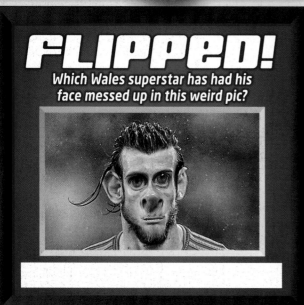

CRAZY KIT!
Which country wore these mad colours in qualifying?

5 QUESTIONS ON...
FRANCE

1 Name the lethal striker who's the only current France player in their all-time top ten goalscorers list!

2 Who is the manager of the France national team - Laurent Blanc, Didier Deschamps or Thierry Henry?

3 Which of these France young guns isn't a defender - Eliaquim Mangala, Raphael Varane or Nabil Fekir?

4 True or False? The Euro 2016 hosts won the European Championship when they last hosted it in 1984!

5 Which of these cities won't host any Euro 2016 matches - Toulouse, Lille, Lens, Bordeaux, Nantes or Nice?

NAME THE TEAM!

Can you name the England starting XI that beat Slovenia 3-2 in their Euro 2016 qualifier?

1. Winger ★ Tottenham

2. Right-back ★ Man. United

3. Centre-back ★ Chelsea

4. Goalkeeper ★ Man. City

5. Centre-back ★ Man. United

6. Midfielder ★ Liverpool

7. Midfielder ★ Man. City

8. Midfielder ★ Arsenal

9. Left-back ★ Arsenal

10. Striker ★ Man. United

Winger ★ Man. City
RAHEEM STERLING

GUESS THE WINNERS!

Which countries won these Euro Championships?

1996

2000

2004

2012

Euro Goal Machines!

Name the countries these stars play for!

1. Robert Lewandowski

2. Gylfi Sigurdsson

3. Kyle Lafferty

4. Rubin Okotie

5. Paco Alcacer

6. Thomas Muller

MATCH! WINNER!

Who scored the only goal in Spain's Euro 2008 Final win against Germany?

ANSWERS

Can you find 40 Euro 2016 qualifying goalscorers in this grid?

Alaba	Damari	Hamsik	Kruse	McGeady	Naismith	Ronaldo	Sigurdsson
Alcacer	Dockal	Huntelaar	Lafferty	Mertens	Novakovic	Rooney	Silva
Bale	Dzeko	Ibrahimovic	Lewandowski	Milik	Pedro	Schurrle	Welbeck
Bendtner	Fellaini	Keane	Maloney	Modric	Perisic	Seferovic	Yarmolenko
Candreva	Fletcher	Kramaric	McClean	Muller	Robben	Shaqiri	Yilmaz

ANSWERS ON PAGE 95

1 How many La Liga goals did the ace attacker score r Atletico Madrid in 014-15 – 18, 20 or 22?

2 Which international tournament was his first for France – World Cup 2010, Euro 2012 or World Cup 2014?

3 Which team didn't the lightning-fast forward score against in La Liga last season – Real Madrid or Barcelona?

4 True or False? The awesome finisher wears the No.10 shirt for the massive Spanish club!

5 The blond-haired goal machine signed for Atletico back in 2014 for £24 million, but from which La Liga club?

FOOTY STARS AS KIDS

MATCH blows the dust off some ancient photo albums and raids footy stars' Instagram accounts to reveal what they looked like when they were younger!

THEO WALCOTT
ARSENAL

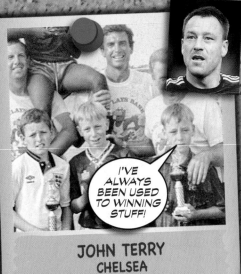

JOHN TERRY
CHELSEA

NEYMAR
BARCELONA

ERIK LAMELA
TOTTENHAM

CARLOS TEVEZ
BOCA JUNIORS

MARIO GOTZE
BAYERN MUNICH

LUKE SHAW
MAN. UNITED

THIAGO SILVA
PSG

CRISTIANO RONALDO
REAL MADRID

STEVEN GERRARD
LA GALAXY

ALEXIS SANCHEZ
ARSENAL

JAMIE CARRAGHER
TV PUNDIT

ROBERTO FIRMINO
LIVERPOOL

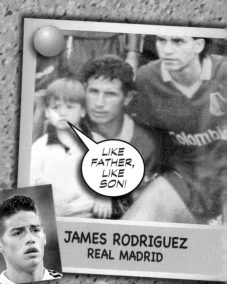

JAMES RODRIGUEZ
REAL MADRID

LIONEL MESSI
BARCELONA

HARRY KANE
TOTTENHAM

DAVID LUIZ
PSG

ASHLEY YOUNG
MAN. UNITED

BOBBY ZAMORA
BRIGHTON

KASPER SCHMEICHEL
LEICESTER

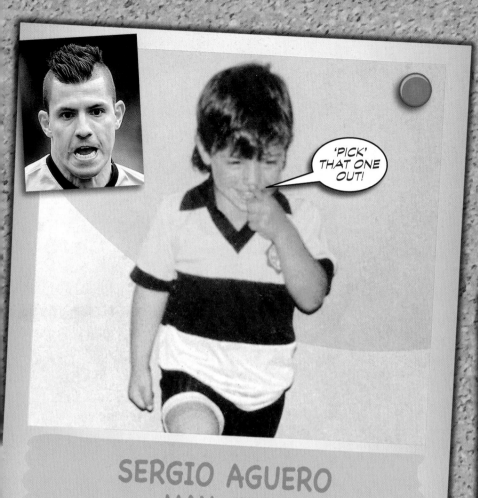

SERGIO AGUERO
MAN. CITY

WAYNE ROONEY
MAN. UNITED

JACK WILSHERE
ARSENAL

FERNANDO TORRES
ATLETICO MADRID

ALEX OXLADE-CHAMBERLAIN
ARSENAL

CESC FABREGAS
CHELSEA

Manchester FIFA derby!

Surely Sergio knows how this one ends?

You'll never eat all that, mate!

SUPERSTARS UNCOVERED No.5

AGUERO

He's a big American Football fan!

Head-to-head with Reus!

With his CL hat-trick ball!

A selfie with Leo!

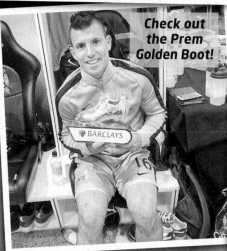

Check out the Prem Golden Boot!

Kun loves Will Smith – he's got him on his T-shirt!

CRAZY STATS & FACTS!

MESSI'S HIS BEZZIE!

Barça and Argentina ledge Lionel Messi is one of Sergio's biggest mates, and godfather to his son!

38

Man. City paid £38 million to sign the deadly striker from Atletico Madrid back in 2011!

26

Aguero scored 26 league goals last season, his best ever total, and won the Prem Golden Boot!

TITLE WINNER!

Aguero's 94th-minute winner against QPR in 2012 sealed City's first-ever Premier League title!

SPECIAL MOVE!

THE QUICK SHOT!

Aguero is the king at taking shots early before keepers can get ready to make a save! He catches them by surprise, and it works!

HOW DOES HE DO IT?

The City star looks around before he gets the ball so he knows where the keeper is, then moves the ball quickly and picks his spot!

BIGGEST BUST-UPS EVER!

Check out some of the most bonkers clashes in footy history!

BATTLE OF OLD TRAFFORD!

Arsenal players were furious with Man. United's Ruud van Nistelrooy in this mega clash back in 2003 - they thought he was diving and faking injury! So when he missed a penalty at the end of the game, some of them got in his face big-time!

HORROR HEADBUTT!

Zinedine Zidane is one of the best footy players ever, but the France legend's career ended badly in the 2006 World Cup Final. He got sent off for headbutting Marco Materazzi and Italy went on to lift the trophy!

DI CANIO GETS PUSHY!

Fiery Sheffield Wednesday star Paolo di Canio shoved a referee to the floor after he was shown a red card against Arsenal in 1998! He was banned for 11 matches and fined £10,000!

WARNING!
DON'T TRY THIS AT HOME!

GAFFER LOSES HIS HEAD!

We couldn't believe it when Alan Pardew headbutted Hull star David Meyler in 2013-14! The ex-Newcastle boss was sent to the stands and later fined a massive £100,000 by The Magpies!

MILLENNIUM MELTDOWN!

Chelsea beat Arsenal 2-1 to win the 2007 League Cup Final, but everyone remembers this match for the massive scraps! Three players were shown red cards, John Terry was knocked out in the second half and there was a big brawl at the end!

GATTUSO SCRAP!

Step aside, Undertaker – Gennaro Gattuso has stolen your finishing move! The Italy legend got a four-match ban after this clash with ex-Spurs assistant Joe Jordan in the 2010-11 Champions League!

MERSEYSIDE MADNESS!

Everton's Francis Jeffers and Liverpool's Sander Westerveld scuffled after collision going for the ball in this 1999 Merseyside derby, and both were given an early bath! It looked more like a boxing match than a game of footy!

BIG MATCH! QUIZ

CHAMPIONS LEAGUE SPECIAL

CAMERA SHY!

Can you name the awesome Champions League gaffers hiding in these pics?

crazy names!

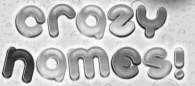

Which Champo League teams have these nicknames?

1. The Dragons

4. The Kids

2. The Wolves

5. The Parisians

3. The Gunners

6. The Old Lady

TRUE or FALSE?

Read these statements and work out if they're true or false!

1. Italian giants AC Milan have qualified for the 2015-16 Champions League!

2. A total of 32 teams play in the group stage of the famous competition!

3. Real Madrid legend Gareth Bale has won the Champions League twice!

4. Two players were shown red cards in the 2015 Champions League Final!

5. The Turkish champions in this season's competition are Galatasaray!

CHAMPIONS LEAGUE HEROES!

A
Atletico Madrid

B
Barcelona

C
Bayern Munich

Philipp Lahm
1

Jackson Martinez
2

Claudio Bravo
3

Match these Champions League stars to the clubs they play for!

MYSTERY MASCOT!

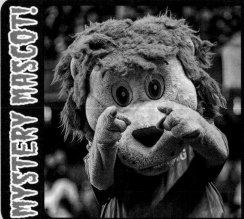

Use the clues to work out which Champions League club this mascot is from!

↘ The animal I look like is known as 'The King Of The Jungle'! Hear me ROAR!

↘ I appear at home games in a class London stadium called Stamford Bridge!

↘ I'm massive mates with Diego, Cesc, John and Eden!

5 QUESTIONS ON...
PSG

1 Which famous stadium do the mega rich club play their home matches at?

2 True or False? They've only won the Champions League once in their entire history!

3 Which national team does superstar striker Zlatan Ibrahimovic play for?

4 Which Premier League team did PSG beat in the knockout stages of last season's Champions League?

5 Can you name the legendary France centre-back who is now the PSG manager?

2011

2012

GUESS THE WINNERS!

Who won the Champions League in these seasons?

2013

2014

1.

2.

3.

🔍 SPOT THE SPONSOR!

Which 2015-16 CL teams have these sponsors on their shirts?

4.

5.

6.

BACK TO THE FUTURE

Which Champions League forward has gone back in time to join a rock band?

ANSWERS ON PAGE 95

BIG '10

Test your knowledge of the Champions League with this rock-solid quiz! Can you get all ten?

4 Which club has won the famous trophy more than anyone else?

1 Neymar, Messi and which other lethal net-buster tied as Champions League top scorers last season?

2 Which Premier League team has won the CL or European Cup more times – Liverpool or Man. United?

3 True or False? Arsenal were the last Premier League team to get to a Champions League final!

6 Bayern scored seven goals against two different teams in the CL last season. Roma was one of them – can you name the other?

5 How many times has Jose Mourinho won the Champions League?

8 Name the last Italian team to win the Champions League!

7 Which three teams were in Man. City's tough Champions League group last season?

'10 Which famous stadium will host the 2016 CL Final?

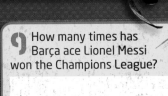

9 How many times has Barça ace Lionel Messi won the Champions League?

ANSWERS ON PAGE 95

NEYMAR

FACTPACK!

Name: Neymar
Age: 23
Position: Forward
Club: Barcelona
Country: Brazil
Strongest Foot: Right
Top Skill: Jaw-dropping tricks!
Value: £85 million
Boots: Nike Hypervenom

WIN!

Put your answers on the entry form in Quiz Answers on page 95 for the chance to win a £50 iTunes voucher!

1 In which Brazilian state was the wicked forward born – Bahia, o Paulo, Rio de Janeiro, rnambuco or Goias?

2 Which one of these trophies hasn't he won – the Spanish Super Cup, Europa League or Confederations Cup?

3 In what year did Barcelona buy the epic trickster from Santos – 2010, 2011, 2012, 2013 or 2014?

4 How many goals did Neymar score at the 2014 World Cup for Brazil – three, four, five, six or seven?

5 Neymar missed the start of the 2015-16 season because of which illness – measles, mumps or chickenpox?

ULTIMATE TEAM LEGENDS
EXPLAINED!

The Legends in *FIFA Ultimate Team* rock, but why are they famous? *MATCH* reveals all!

MALDINI
CB ★ OVR 92

Paolo Maldini **must live in a big house, because** he needs a massive trophy cabinet to store everything he's won! The classy centre-back, who was also a top LB, played for AC Milan his whole career and picked up 26 trophies, including five European Cups. Oh, and he captained Italy over 70 times!

MALDINI		
92 CB		
BASIC		
86 PAC	67 DRI	
56 SHO	95 DEF	
74 PAS	80 PHY	

BIGGEST TROPHIES

European Cup/CL	5
Serie A	7
Coppa Italia	1
Supercoppa Italiana	5
UEFA Super Cup	5

SCHMEICHEL
GK ★ OVR 90

SCHMEICHEL		
90 GK		
BASIC		
88 DIV	93 REF	
82 HAN	53 SPE	
83 KIC	85 POS	

Man. United fans love giant keeper Peter Schmeichel – **mostly because** he helped The Red Devils win the treble in 1999, including the Champions League! He was class at international level too, and starred as Denmark won the Euros in 1992! His bravery and ability to save one-on-ones was epic!

BIGGEST TROPHIES

Euro Championship	1
Champions League	1
Premier League	5
FA Cup	3
League Cup	1

VIEIRA
CM ★ OVR 88

Patrick Vieira **was a real winner!** He led Arsenal's famous invincibles team, won three Prem titles and bossed the league for years with his monster tackling, surging runs and slick passing. Did we mention the all-action CM also won the 1998 World Cup with France and Euro 2000 two years later?

VIEIRA		
88 CM		
BASIC		
84 PAC	82 DRI	
71 SHO	85 DEF	
79 PAS	91 PHY	

BIGGEST TROPHIES

World Cup	1
Euro Championship	1
Premier League	3
Serie A	4
FA Cup	5

PELE
CF ★ OVR 95

Legends don't get more legendary than this guy! Pele is the only player in footy history to win THREE World Cups, he scored over 1,000 goals in his career and won more club and individual trophies than MATCH can count! It's no surprise his nickname was 'The King Of Football'!

PELÉ	
95 CF	
🇧🇷	BASIC
95 PAC	94 DRI
89 SHO	53 DEF
89 PAS	73 PHY

BIGGEST TROPHIES

World Cup	
Copa Libertadores	
Intercontinental Cup	2
Intercont. Supercup	
Brasileiro Serie A	6

ZOLA
CF ★ OVR 87

ZOLA	
87 CF	
🇮🇹	BASIC
85 PAC	89 DRI
82 SHO	32 DEF
84 PAS	62 PHY

BIGGEST TROPHIES

UEFA Cup	1
UEFA Cup Winners' Cup	1
Serie A	1
FA Cup	2
League Cup	1

Gianfranco Zola lit up the Prem for Chelsea with his top-class technique, clever footy brain, lethal finishing and bending free-kicks! He could play up front or out wide and always made something special happen, which is why he's still talked about as one of the Prem's best players ever!

LAUDRUP
CAM ★ OVR 89

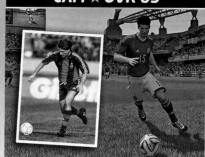

You might only know Michael Laudrup as the ex-manager of Swansea, but as a player he was one of the most exciting footballers on the planet! He played inch-perfect passes, tied defenders in knots with his dribbling and ripped the net with lethal finishes! He rocked for Real Madrid and Barça!

LAUDRUP	
89 CAM	
🇩🇰	BASIC
85 PAC	89 DRI
73 SHO	38 DEF
87 PAS	64 PHY

BIGGEST TROPHIES

European Cup	
La Liga	5
Serie A	1
Eredivisie	1
UEFA Super Cup	

BERGKAMP
CF ★ OVR 90

Dennis Bergkamp had a crazy scoring record for Ajax, won the UEFA Cup with Inter then moved to Arsenal and truly became a legend! He picked up three titles, was part of the invincibles team and scored one of the best Prem goals ever! Search 'Bergkamp Newcastle' on YouTube now to check it out!

BERGKAMP	
90 CF	
🇳🇱	BASIC
83 PAC	87 DRI
90 SHO	29 DEF
83 PAS	79 PHY

BIGGEST TROPHIES

Premier League	
UEFA Cup	
FA Cup	4
Eredivisie	
UEFA Cup Winners' Cup	

OKOCHA
CAM ★ OVR 87

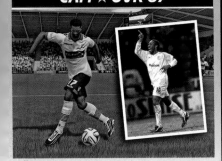

OKOCHA	
87 CAM	
BASIC	
84 PAC	90 DRI
80 SHO	35 DEF
81 PAS	58 PHY

When Okocha got on the ball, you knew something special was going to happen! He had the tricks to make defenders look silly, and busted them out for fun at Bolton and PSG! He's one of Nigeria's best-ever players, and fans used to say that Jay-Jay was so good they named him twice!

BIGGEST TROPHIES

Olympic Gold	1
Africa Cup Of Nations	1
Intertoto Cup	1
Trophee des Champions	1
Championship Play-Off	1

DESAILLY
CB ★ OVR 89

DESAILLY	
89 CB	
BASIC	
82 PAC	66 DRI
51 SHO	88 DEF
64 PAS	88 PHY

You've probably seen Marcel Desailly as a TV pundit, but did you know he's one of the best defenders ever? He won the CL with Marseille, bagged just about every trophy going with AC Milan then played over 150 Prem games for Chelsea! He also won two small things called the WORLD CUP and the EUROS!

BIGGEST TROPHIES

World Cup	
Euro Championship	1
Champions League	2
Serie A	2
FA Cup	

ROBERTO CARLOS
LB ★ OVR 88

ROBERTO CARLOS	
88 LB	
BASIC	
91 PAC	79 DRI
81 SHO	82 DEF
84 PAS	85 PHY

If you haven't seen Roberto Carlos' banana free-kick against France in 1997, check it out because you won't believe your eyes! There was more to his game than crazy free-kicks, though – he was ace in defence and attack for Real Madrid and Brazil! He's one of the best-left backs ever!

BIGGEST TROPHIES

World Cup	
Champions League	
Copa America	2
La Liga	
Intercontinental Cup	2

GULLIT
CM ★ OVR 90

GULLIT	
90 CM	
BASIC	
86 PAC	86 DRI
83 SHO	79 DEF
89 PAS	82 PHY

In his playing days, Ruud Gullit was a powerhouse midfielder who could dominate games at the highest level! He became the most expensive player in the world when he moved from PSV to AC Milan for £6 million in 1987, and won the Ballon d'Or before captaining Holland to Euro 88 glory!

BIGGEST TROPHIES

Euro Championship	1
European Cup	2
Serie A	3
FA Cup	1
Eredivisie	3

BECKENBAUER
CB ★ OVR 93

BECKENBAUER	
93 CB	
BASIC	
82 PAC	79 DRI
69 SHO	94 DEF
83 PAS	81 PHY

Of all the great players that Germany have produced, Franz Beckenbauer is probably the best ever! Known as 'Der Kaiser' – which means 'The Emperor' – he led West Germany to World Cup glory in 1974. He bossed it with Bayern, too – he played over 500 games and won the European Cup three times!

BIGGEST TROPHIES

World Cup	
Euro Championship	
European Cup	
Bundesliga	
DFB-Pokal German Cup	

MATTHAUS
CDM ★ OVR 91

MATTHÄUS
91 | CDM
BASIC

86 PAC	77 DRI
86 SHO	88 DEF
86 PAS	82 PHY

BIGGEST TROPHIES

World Cup	
Euro Championship	
UEFA Cup	
Bundesliga	
Serie A	

Germany's Lothar Matthaus played in a record five World Cups and is still his country's most-capped player ever! He was also the first-ever FIFA World Player Of The Year and is the only German player to win it! Matthaus spent most of his club career with Bayern and won SEVEN league titles!

FOWLER
ST ★ OVR 86

FOWLER
86 | ST
BASIC

83 PAC	83 DRI
82 SHO	48 DEF
73 PAS	76 PHY

BIGGEST TROPHIES

UEFA Cup	1
FA Cup	1
League Cup	2
UEFA Super Cup	1
Charity Shield	1

Robbie Fowler played for tons of clubs in his career, but he's most famous for his time at Liverpool where he earned the nickname 'God' – the fans couldn't get enough of his goals! He was one of England's most lethal finishers ever and beat keepers with power shots, finesse finishes and cheeky chips!

MOORE
CB ★ OVR 88

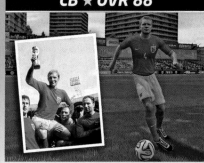

MOORE
88 | CB
BASIC

77 PAC	74 DRI
62 SHO	87 DEF
79 PAS	84 PHY

BIGGEST TROPHIES

World Cup	
FA Cup	
UEFA Cup Winners' Cup	
Int. Soccer League	
Euro Bronze	

Bobby Moore is one of the greatest England players of all time and led The Three Lions to their historic World Cup victory in 1966! He won over 100 international caps, played over 600 games for West Ham and legendary striker Pele says he's the toughest defender he ever faced!

VAN BASTEN
ST ★ OVR 91

VAN BASTEN
91 | ST
BASIC

83 PAC	80 DRI
94 SHO	34 DEF
73 PAS	70 PHY

BIGGEST TROPHIES

Euro Championship	
European Cup	
Serie A	
Eredivisie	
UEFA Super Cup	

If Marco van Basten hadn't retired early because of injury, he might have broken every scoring record around! He hit 128 goals in 133 league games for Ajax before joining AC Milan, where he won three Ballon d'Or awards and FIFA World Player Of The Year! MVB was the ultimate goal machine!

Chilling on the plane with big pal, Pepe!

Ron's born for modelling – he just loves posing!

That is one wicked bike!

SUPERSTARS UNCOVERED No.6

RONALDO

He pranked a team-mate by covering his car in foil!

Boxing legend Floyd Mayweather Jr is a mate!

With his third Ballon d'Or!

Nice wheels, give us a lift!

Digital Ron and Hugo The Troll!

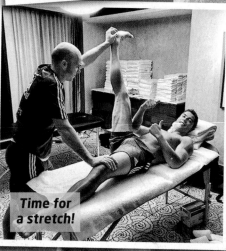

Time for a stretch!

CRAZY STATS & FACTS!

Real Madrid paid £80 million to sign Ron in 2009 – the biggest transfer fee ever at the time!

80

THE MUSEUM OF RON!

Yep - Ronaldo's got his own museum! It's on the island of Madeira where he was born, and it's packed with trophies!

27

Ronaldo holds the record for the most number of hat-tricks in La Liga!

MR. POPULAR!

Cristiano is the first footballer ever to reach 100 million fans on Facebook - that's even more than MATCH!

SPECIAL MOVE!

THE HEEL CHOP!

Ron uses this mega flash move to quickly change direction and beat a defender! It takes timing, skill, agility and lots of practice!

HOW DOES HE DO IT?

He does a jump and puts one foot behind the other, then uses the inside of his foot to push the ball where he wants to go!

SNAPPED!
BEST OF 2015! PART TWO

Martial arts expert!

MY KARATE CHOPS ARE LETHAL!

Hair scare!

Has Maicon spotted bird poo in Muller's barnet?

NAH, IT'S JUST HAIR GEL, MATE!

Eye Spy!

This game's all over for Gestede!

SOMETHING BEGINNING WITH 'B'!

Golden oldie!

We're not sure about Palace's new striker!

I'VE GOT A £20M PRICE TAG!

Wenger's new boy!

Arsenal's star signing loves flying down the wing!

JUST CALL ME DANNY WEL-BEAK. LOL!

Toffees time machine!

"THIS IS WELL WEIRD!"

"NOW IT'S TIME FOR THE TANGO!"

Groovin' gaffer!

Luis Enrique just can't get enough of Strictly Come Dancing!

Ron's in trouble!

Cristiano's been made to sit on the naughty step!

"CAN I GO NOW, PLEASE? I'M BURSTING!"

Wrestle Kane-ia!

Harry Kane is a big fan of WWE!

Sanch's mega selfie!

"THIS IS GOING STRAIGHT ON INSTAGRAM, MATCH!"

TOP 10

TRANSFERS THAT NEARLY HAPPENED!

*NOT ALL OF THESE PICS ARE REAL!

10 ROBERT LEWANDOWSKI
Lech Poznan to Blackburn
2010

Lewa was going to sign for Blackburn until an ash cloud meant his flight got cancelled, so he joined Dortmund instead!

9 ANDRIY SHEVCHENKO
Dynamo Kiev to West Ham
1995

Harry Redknapp nearly signed a young Ukraine striker, until he found out he'd have to pay £1 million and changed his mind. That player was Shevchenko!

6 ZLATAN IBRAHIMOVIC
Ajax to Arsenal
2000

Young Ajax star Ibrahimovic could have signed for The Gunners back in 2000, but he refused to take part in a trial! 'Zlatan doesn't do auditions', he reckoned!

8 RADAMEL FALCAO
River Plate to Aston Villa
2008

Martin O'Neill was offered young River Plate striker Falcao for £5 million, but chose to buy Emile Heskey instead!

7 GARETH BALE
Tottenham to Nott'm Forest
2009

It's hard to believe, but Harry Redknapp nearly sold Bale to Forest for £3 million!

MOTCHI

5

STEVEN GERRARD
Liverpool to Chelsea
2005

Stevie G was close to joining Chelsea just weeks after winning the Champions League, but changed his mind at the last minute!

4

CRISTIANO RONALDO
Sporting to Arsenal
2003

Arsenal almost snapped up Ron – he visited their training ground and was even given a shirt with his name on the back!

ZINEDINE ZIDANE
Bordeaux to Blackburn
1995

3

Rovers could have bagged Zizou, but chairman Jack Walker said they already had Tim Sherwood and didn't need him!

RONALDINHO
Gremio to St. Mirren
2001

2

Just before moving to PSG, Ron wanted to spend time in Europe to get used to the weather and almost joined Scottish side St. Mirren. Wow!

1

LIONEL MESSI
Barcelona to Arsenal
2003

Arsene Wenger nearly signed Cesc Fabregas, Gerard Pique and Messi all at once! Leo was up for it but work permit problems ended the move. Gutted!

100% FOOTY ACTION EVERY WEEK!

MATCH!

PLANET NEYMAR!

MASSIVE INTERVIEW!
STERLING!
CITY'S £49 MILLION SUPERSTAR!

"I'm looking forward to working with Sergio Aguero!"

THE BIGGEST STARS!

SUPER MESSI!

MATCH checks out the BARÇA legend's epic skills, shows you how to play like him and reveals his craziest stats!

FACE SWAP!

MATCH has switched around loads of faces, just for the LOLs!

AWESOME FEATURES!

FUNNY PICS!

  LIKE MATCH AT... FACEBOOK.COM/MATCHMAGAZINE

EXTRA-TIME

Reckon your footy knowledge is off the charts? Find out by tackling these tricky brain-teasers!

1 Which legendary Man. United star took charge as manager for a while after David Moyes was sacked in 2014?

2 Name the country Dortmund striker Pierre-Emerick Aubameyang plays for!

3 Which Bundesliga club did Liverpool sign Brazil ace Roberto Firmino from in the summer transfer window?

4 True or False? Chelsea's Prem title win in 2014-15 was their third in total!

5 Which Spanish club are nicknamed Los Blancos – Real Madrid or Levante?

6 Which club did PSG sign star striker Zlatan Ibrahimovic from in 2012?

7 Who has won more England caps – Jordan Henderson or Jack Wilshere?

8 What's the name of Atletico Madrid's famous stadium – Bernabeu, Vicente Calderon, Nou Camp or Mestalla?

9 Can you remember which country knocked the England Women's team out of the 2015 World Cup in Canada?

10 Which awesome attacking star wears the number 17 shirt for Arsenal?

11 Who did Tim Sherwood replace as the Aston Villa manager?

12 Which epic striker was the Premier League's top goalscorer last season?

13 True or False? Romelu Lukaku is Everton's record signing!

14 Which national team does midfielder Morgan Schneiderlin play for?

15 Which Juventus player scored in last season's Champions League final against Barcelona?

16 And can you name all three of Barça's scorers in that match?

17 How old is Southampton striker Graziano Pelle – 25, 28 or 30?

18 Which team finished second in the Bundesliga in 2014-15?

19 Which Premier League side are nicknamed The Saints?

20 Rock-solid defender Sebastian Coates joined Sunderland from which club last summer – Liverpool or QPR?

21 Which team conceded more Prem goals in 2014-15 – Tottenham or Hull?

22 What first name links Morrison, Rodriguez and McArthur?

23 Watford play their home games at which wicked stadium?

24 Name the rapid striker who was top scorer in France's Ligue 1 last season!

25 Which national team does Real Madrid pass master Toni Kroos play for?

ANSWERS ON PAGE 95

MATCH!
THE BEST FOOTBALL MAGAZINE!

FACTPACK!

Name: *Gareth Bale*
Age: *26*
Position: *Winger*
Club: *Real Madrid*
Country: *Wales*
Strongest Foot: Left
Top Skill: Wicked long shots!
Value: *£100 million*
Boots: *Adidas X15*

BALE

WIN!

Put your answers on the entry form in Quiz Answers on page 95 for the chance to win a £50 iTunes voucher!

1 Which massive Italian club did the Wales legend score his first-ever professional hat-trick against in 2010?

2 What position did the wicked winger start his career at for Southampton – left-back or defensive midfielder?

3 He scored in the 2014 Champions League Final – did he bag Real's first, second, third or fourth goal?

4 True or False? His uncle used to play for Championship clubs Cardiff and Fulham as a striker!

5 How many goals did the ace winger score for Tottenham in the Premier League – 29, 36, 42 or 49?

Adidas have their own boot model just for Messi!

Coolest team shot ever?

With Argentina pals Di Maria and Lavezzi!

SUPERSTARS UNCOVERED No.7

MESSI

Not many people have a pair of these bad boys!

Another CL trophy to add to the collection!

Epic fashion fail, Leo!

Chilling in the pool!

Hanging out with Barça pals!

Inside the Nou Camp dressing room!

CRAZY STATS & FACTS!

He once hit 73 goals in all comps for Barça – no player has ever scored more in one season for a club in Europe's top divisions!

73

CRAZY CONTRACT!

He joined Barcelona when he was just 13 years old, and his first contract was written on a paper napkin!

4

Leo has won four Ballon d'Or awards – that's more than any other player, ever! Oh, and they were all in a row!

THE FLEA!

His nickname is 'La Pulga', which translates as 'The Flea'!

SPECIAL MOVE!

THE SWITCH!

Messi doesn't do tricks, but he's still one of footy's best dribblers because he can switch direction in an instant AND keep the ball!

HOW DOES HE DO IT?

The lethal forward slows down, waits for the defender to commit, then quickly nudges the ball away at an angle and accelerates off!

ATTACKING SUPERSTARS... WHO ARE YOU?

Take the MATCH quiz to find out!

1. What kind of tricks have you got in your locker?

A I'm not into tricks, I beat players with dribbling and changes of direction!

B Any trick I like – I'm so good at them, I make them up when I'm out there!

C There isn't a trick on the planet I can't do! I'm the king of sick skills!

D My locker is pretty much empty of tricks – that's not really my style, MATCH!

2. If you raced your team-mates, where would you finish?

A I'd burn away at first, but might get caught up!

B I reckon I'd be right up there with the leaders!

C First. I've got to be the quickest player ever!

D My brain is fast, but my legs aren't that rapid. I'd probably be somewhere in the middle of the pack!

3. You're one-on-one with the keeper... what happens next?

A I work out the best place to put the ball and that's where it goes – there's no messing about with me!

B I'd probably lob him. That or invent a completely new way to bust the net!

C I think you know. The keeper picks the ball out of the net and my celebrations begin! I do not miss chances.

D I pick my spot and shoot before the keeper knows what's going on! Gooooaall!!

4. What boots do you usually wear?

A I've got my own brand of boots. Beat that!

B I like Nike boots the best, so I'll go with them!

C That's easy. I've worn Mercurial or Superfly boots for my whole career!

D It's got to be the Nike Hypervenoms for me!

5. Where do you play?

A They named the false nine position after me! I can also play in a front three!

B I'm an old-fashioned winger with epic skills!

C Anywhere. Play me where you like – I'll still score!

D Get the ball to me in the box and I'll do the rest!

6. What's your passing ability like, then?

A I get tons of assists! Setting team-mates up is almost as much fun as scoring!

B My crosses are ridiculous, and I can pick any of my team-mates out with passes that no-one expects to see!

C I pass if I need to for the team, but I'd rather hit the back of the net myself!

D I'm ace at holding the ball up and bringing my pals into play with clever touches!

MOSTLY A
MESSI

You've got speed, brains, vision, skills and lethal finishing ability, just like the best player ever! Are you sure you're not a professional footballer already?

MOSTLY B
BOLASIE

Everyone loves watching you play! You're totally unique and always come up with flash moves and awesome skills no-one else has ever thought of. You rock!

MOSTLY C
RONALDO

When people ask who the best player is at your school, there's only one answer! You're the top dog and everyone knows it. Your game is epic!

MOSTLY D
KANE

Anyone order goals? That's where you come in! You're not interested in tricks and you don't have lightning pace, but you make finding the net look easy!